职业教育汽车类专业"互联网+"创新教材

Automobile Business English
汽车商务英语

第3版

主　编　张素容　肖　婷
副主编　侯玲玲　郑　怡　梅加元
参　编　周　明　何小青　芦开智　赵福花　王丽红
　　　　马　翀　常海艳
主　审　归艳荣

机械工业出版社

本书共有两大模块。模块一：汽车英语，共有11课，主要以图表的形式，从汽车类型，汽车发动机，汽车底盘，汽车电气系统，汽车车身，燃油经济性、安全配置、舒适配置与操纵性，新能源汽车方面讲述了汽车核心词汇和知识，内容生动形象，练习浅显易懂。模块二：商务英语，共有12课，讲述了在汽车销售及售后领域开展业务的12个方面，主要内容包括客户开发，客户接待，信息收集，汽车介绍，价格协商，车辆交付，支付方式，投诉处理，用户反馈，维修接待，汽车维护和汽车保险。为了便于教学，本书附有汽车标志、参考译文、汽车专业词汇和常用词汇。

本书可作为职业院校汽车类专业教材，也可供从事汽车商务工作的相关人员参考与学习。

凡选用本书作为授课教材的教师，均可登录 www.cmpedu.com 下载配套电子课件和习题答案，或来电咨询：010-88379375。同时还配有示范教学包，可在超星学习通上实现"一键建课"，方便混合式教学。

图书在版编目（CIP）数据

汽车商务英语/张素容，肖婷主编．—3版．—北京：机械工业出版社，2021.9（2025.6重印）

职业教育汽车类专业"互联网+"创新教材

ISBN 978-7-111-68896-9

Ⅰ.①汽… Ⅱ.①张…②肖… Ⅲ.①汽车-商务-英语-职业教育-教材 Ⅳ.①F766

中国版本图书馆 CIP 数据核字（2021）第 157902 号

机械工业出版社（北京市百万庄大街22号 邮政编码100037）
策划编辑：曹新宇 责任编辑：曹新宇
责任校对：蓝伙金 封面设计：鞠 杨
责任印制：单爱军
中煤（北京）印务有限公司印刷
2025年6月第3版第5次印刷
184mm×260mm·12.5印张·245千字
标准书号：ISBN 978-7-111-68896-9
定价：45.00元

电话服务 网络服务
客服电话：010-88361066 机 工 官 网：www.cmpbook.com
　　　　　010-88379833 机 工 官 博：weibo.com/cmp1952
　　　　　010-68326294 金 书 网：www.golden-book.com
封底无防伪标均为盗版 机工教育服务网：www.cmpedu.com

第3版前言

　　当今世界高新技术快速发展，汽车逐步成为高新技术高度集中的现代化产品。随着新能源和智能驾驶技术在汽车领域的普及，职业教育信息化的程度不断提升，教材编写需要与时俱进，以适应快速发展的汽车产业和不断更新的职业院校汽车类专业人才培养需要，为此我们对《汽车商务英语》进行第三次修订。本书根据企业对应用型技术人才在汽车相关专业方面的技能要求，结合汽车新技术的发展趋势，将原教材内容加以取舍、整合，以汽车专业英语为基础、以商务英语为主线，将发动机、底盘、电气系统、新能源汽车与汽车营销、汽车维修、汽车保险等相关内容有机结合在一起，运用信息化手段改编成全新的教材。编写过程中，我们坚持"必学够用原则"，突出培养学生"核心素养"理念，并强化教材信息化程度，使得本教材既能满足教师混合式教学需要，又能满足学生泛在学习需要；此外，还融入了新能源汽车、汽车燃油经济性等内容。主要内容分为两个模块。

　　模块一：汽车英语部分，由原来的13课调整为11课，内容包括：汽车类型，汽车发动机，汽车底盘，汽车电气系统，汽车车身，燃油经济性，安全配置、舒适配置与操纵性，新能源汽车。

　　模块二：商务英语部分，由原来的13课调整为12课，内容包括：客户开发、客户接待、信息收集、汽车介绍、价格商议、车辆交付、支付方式、投诉处理、用户反馈、维修接待、汽车维护和汽车保险。

　　本书尽量避免理论过深、专业性太强及与实际应用关系不大的内容，符合汽车类相关专业职业教育人才的培养目标和职业教育的特点。本书各章节相对独立，不同专业可根据具体的教学需要进行调整和取舍。

　　本书由武汉机电工程学校张素容和肖婷主编。除原编写者外，武汉交通学校侯玲玲和周明、武汉机电工程学校的郑怡和梅加元，也加入到编写团队中，为本次改编带来新鲜力量。在编写过程中，要感谢机械工业出版社给予我们的支持和鼓励，感谢武汉超星公司对本书信息化内容的拍摄支持，感谢东风风神武汉吉亨 4S 店提供的专业指导及拍摄辅助。

由于编者水平有限，书中难免有不妥之处，恳请读者和同行批评指正。

编　者

第2版前言

　　随着汽车工业的快速发展，汽车正以其前所未有的速度走进千家万户，改变着人们的生活。在汽车普及浪潮愈演愈烈的背景下，在汽车日益成为人类生活新伙伴的今天，汽车及汽车商务人才在人才市场已然成为供不应求的紧缺型技能人才。为满足汽车人才市场的需要以及配合各职业技术学校汽车及汽车商务专业的课程开设，2008年我们开始编写《汽车商务英语》教材。本教材针对职业院校学生英语基础差、水平参差不齐的特点，贯彻"必需，够用"的原则和"以应用为主线，以能力为中心"的指导思想，改革传统的课程体系，采用模块式教学方式编写，注重分层教学，中英文对照，图文并茂，使教材形式更新颖，内容更浅显生动。经过几年的使用与反馈，为了使本教材内容更加实用，我们对本教材了进行修订。主要修订内容如下。

　　模块一：由原来的11课调整为13课，主要以图表的形式从汽车类型，汽车发动机，汽车底盘，汽车电气系统，汽车车身，汽车尺寸和重量，汽车性能、外观和内饰，汽车安全配置，汽车舒适配置等方面讲述了汽车核心词汇和基础知识。修订之后加强了汽车发动机、底盘和电气系统专业英语知识的编写，使得本书更具专业性。

　　模块二：汽车商务知识，共13课，讲述了在汽车销售及售后领域开展业务的十三个方面，主要内容包括客户接待、客户开发、信息收集、汽车介绍、价格协商、交易促成、支付方式、用户反馈、投诉处理、维修接待、汽车维护和汽车保险。这一模块除了对用词选择、问题设置等方面进行了修改，还在每一课的最后增加了学生的自测部分。为了便于教学和自学，在附录部分除了原来的参考译文、专业词汇和常用词汇外，还增加了汽车标志内容。

　　本书由武汉机电工程学校张素容和何小青担任主编，北京汽车工业学校赵福花、武汉机电工程学校肖婷、芦开智担任副主编。原书的模块一第1至6课由北京汽车工业学校的赵福花、王丽红、马翀、常海燕编写，第7至11课由武汉机电工程学校的何小青编写。原书模块二第 1 至 7 课由芦开智编写，第 8 至 12 课由张素容编写，第 13 课由肖婷编写。本书在修订过程中汽车英语部分由张素容、何小青、芦开智具体改编，商务英语部分由肖婷改编。本书由天津交通学院归艳荣主审。修订之后本书加强了汽车的专业英语内容，使得本书不仅适用于汽车商务专业的学生学习，还适合所有汽车专业学生的英语学习。本书模块一和模块二建议分别以 30 个教学课时完成。

由于编者水平和经验有限，书中难免有不妥和错误之处，恳请读者和同行批评指正。

编　者

第1版前言

随着汽车工业的快速发展,买车、学车、修车、赛车不断升温。汽车正以前所未有的速度改变着人们的生活,吸引着越来越多人的热切目光。在汽车日益普及、逐步成为人类生活新伙伴的今天,汽车技术人才和汽车商务人才奇缺。为满足汽车销售市场的需要、配合各职业技术院校汽车及汽车商务专业的课程需求,我们组织编写了本书。

本书针对职业院校学生英语基础差、水平参差不齐的特点,贯彻"必需,够用"的原则和"以应用为主线,以能力为中心"的指导思想,改革传统的课程体系,采用模块式教学方式编写,注重分层教学,中英文对照,图文并茂,使教材形式更新颖,内容更浅显生动。

本书共两大模块。

模块一:汽车英语,共11课,主要以图表的形式,从汽车类型,汽车结构,汽车发动机,汽车底盘,汽车电气系统,汽车车身、尺寸和重量,汽车性能,外观和内饰,汽车安全配置,汽车舒适配置几个方面讲述了汽车基础核心词汇和知识。

模块二:商务英语,共13课,讲述在汽车销售及售后领域开展业务的几个方面,主要包括客户接待、客户开发、信息收集、汽车介绍、价格协商、促成交易、支付方式、处理投诉、用户反馈、维修接待、汽车维护和汽车保险。为了便于教学,本书附有参考译文。

本书由武汉机电工程学校张素容和何小青任主编,北京汽车工业学校赵福花、武汉机电工程学校芦开智任副主编。本书第一模块第1~6课由北京汽车工业学校赵福花、王丽红、马翀、常海燕编写;第7~11课由武汉机电工程学校何小青编写。第二模块第12~18课由芦开智编写,第19~23课由张素容编写,第24课由武汉机电工程学校肖婷编写。本书由天津交通学院归艳荣主审。

由于编者水平和经验有限,书中难免有不妥之处,恳请读者和同行批评指正。

编　者

Contents 目录

第 3 版前言
第 2 版前言
第 1 版前言

Module One Automobile English 汽车英语 ································· 1
- Lesson 1 Automobile Types ··· 3
- Lesson 2 Automobile Engine Ⅰ ·· 8
- Lesson 3 Automobile Engine Ⅱ ·· 14
- Lesson 4 Automobile Chassis Ⅰ ··· 20
- Lesson 5 Automobile Chassis Ⅱ ··· 26
- Lesson 6 Automobile Electrical System Ⅰ ···································· 32
- Lesson 7 Automobile Electrical System Ⅱ ···································· 38
- Lesson 8 Automobile Body ·· 43
- Lesson 9 Fuel Economy ·· 48
- Lesson 10 Automobile Safety, Comfortable Equipment and Maneuverability ········ 53
- Lesson 11 New Energy Vehicles ··· 59

Module Two Business English 商务英语 ································· 65
- Lesson 1 Customer Development ·· 67
- Lesson 2 Customer Reception ·· 74
- Lesson 3 Information Collection ·· 80
- Lesson 4 Automobile Introduction ·· 86
- Lesson 5 Price Discussion ··· 93
- Lesson 6 Delivery of Vehicles ·· 99
- Lesson 7 Terms of Payment ··· 107
- Lesson 8 Settling Complaints ·· 114
- Lesson 9 Customer Feedback ··· 121
- Lesson 10 Maintenance Reception ··· 128

| Lesson 11 | Vehicle Maintenance | 135 |
| Lesson 12 | Motor Insurance | 142 |

附录 … 149
  附录A 汽车标志 … 151
  附录B 参考译文 … 154
  附录C 汽车专业词汇 … 173
  附录D 常用词汇 … 180

参考文献 … 187

Module One
Automobile English

汽车英语

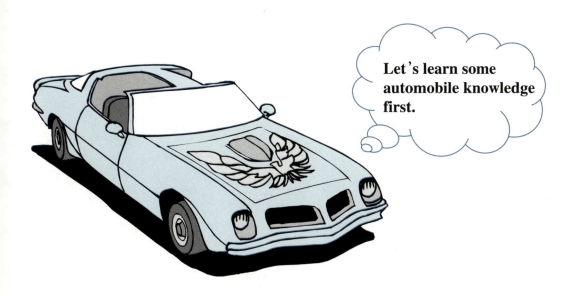

Let's learn some automobile knowledge first.

Module One Automobile English 汽车英语

Lesson 1

Automobile Types

Learning Objectives

Master the basic knowledge and skills	
➢ Language learning objective	Grasp the new words about the common vehicles.
➢ Skill learning objectives	1. Identify different types of vehicles in English. 2. Know the classification of vehicles.
Develop core competences of English	

➢ Develop the ability to search for information about various vehicles on the Internet.
➢ Develop the positive attitude to overcome obstacles in English learning.
➢ Develop image recognition ability in workplace.
➢ Develop the abilities of self-assessment and self-improvement efficiently.

Part One: Warming-up

Look at the pictures and select the right name to each one from the given names.

Fig. 1-1　Automobile types

　　sedan 轿车　　coupe 双门轿车　　convertible 敞篷轿车　　station wagon 厢式轿车　　coach 旅游轿车
　　jeep 吉普车　　truck 货车　　tractor 拖拉机　　crane car 吊车　　refrigerator truck 冷藏车　　mixer truck 搅拌车
　　fire-engine 消防车　　snowplow 铲雪车　　ambulance 救护车　　double-decker bus 双层巴士

> There are many kinds of vehicles all over the world, and they can be classified into 3 groups:
> 1. Recreational and off-road vehicles;
> 2. Passenger sedans and light commercial vehicles;
> 3. Heavy vehicles.

Part Two: Text

Types of Vehicles

There are many kinds of vehicles all over the world, and they can <u>be classified into</u> 3 groups. Within each of these groups, there are many different **classifications** and they can be **described** <u>as follows</u>.

1. Recreational and off-road vehicles

Recreational vehicles <u>are capable of</u> traveling long distances <u>for</u> recreational <u>purpose</u>. **Off-road vehicles** like jeeps, **SUVs** are often used on roads <u>in poor condition</u>.

2. Passenger sedans and light commercial vehicles

Passenger sedans are used by households in everyday situations. They can carry 4~6 persons. This group also **includes** light **commercial vehicles** like light pick-up vehicles which are used to carry light **loads**.

3. Heavy vehicles

Trucks <u>belong to</u> heavy vehicles. Generally, they are made for carrying heavy loads. **Articulated vehicles** and **tipping vehicles** also belong to this type. Buses are another type of heavy vehicles. <u>According to</u> their length and design, buses can also <u>be classified into</u> small, **medium**, large and articulated buses. **Agricultural vehicles** are another type of heavy vehicles, like **tractors**.

In addition, there are many other **special** types of heavy vehicles <u>such as</u> street **water sprinklers**, **ambulances** and **fire-engines** (fire-trucks). They serve us <u>in our daily life</u>.

Sidebar vocabulary:

- be classified into 可分成……
- classification 类别
- describe 描述
- as follows 如下
- recreational vehicle 旅行车
- for... purpose 以……为目的
- off-road vehicle 越野车
- be capable of 能够……
- in poor condition 在恶劣的条件下
- passenger 乘客
- include 包括
- commercial vehicle 商用车
- load 荷载
- belong to 属于
- according to 根据
- be classified as 归类为
- medium 中型的
- agricultural vehicle 农用车
- special 特殊的
- such as 例如
- in our daily life 在我们的日常生活中

Module One Automobile English 汽车英语

Part Three: Words Study

sedan 轿车	crane car 吊车
coupe 双门轿车	refrigerator truck 冷藏车
convertible 敞篷轿车	mixer truck 搅拌车
coach 旅游轿车	fire-engine 消防车
agriculture vehicle 农用车	articulated vehicle 铰接车，拖车
truck 货车	tipping vehicle 自卸车
tractor 拖拉机	water sprinkler 洒水车
snowplow 铲雪车	double-decker bus 双层巴士
ambulance 救护车	SUV 运动型多功能车
police car 警车	off-road vehicle 越野车
station wagon 厢式轿车	recreational vehicle 休闲车

Part Four: Knowledge Extension

I. What are we? Write out our Chinese and English names.

Jeep
吉普车

fire-engine
消防车

sedan
轿车

station wagon
厢式轿车

ambulance
救护车

van
货车

double-decker bus
双层巴士

car
汽车

clean vehicle
清洁车

| coupe | truck | convertible |
| 双门轿车 | 卡车 | 敞篷车 |

| tipping vehicle | tractor | crane car |
| 自卸车 | 拖拉机 | 吊车 |

Part Five: Practice

Ⅰ. Find out the words.

sedancoachjeeptrucktractorcranecarmixertruck

fireengineambulancepolicecarbusstationwagon

Ⅱ. Classify the following (Fig. 1-2) vehicles.

1. Recreational and off-road vehicles: _____

Fig. 1-2　Practice Ⅱ

2. Passenger sedans and light commercial vehicles：
_____

3. Heavy vehicles：_____

Ⅲ. Words puzzle.

s _ d _ n   j _ _ p   tr _ ct _ r
m _ x _ r tr _ ck   _ mbul _ nce   sn _ _ pl _ w
c _ _ ch   tr _ ck   cr _ ne c _ r
f _ re _ ng _ ne   p _ l _ cec _ r   st _ tion w _ g _ n

Ⅳ. Complete the words map.

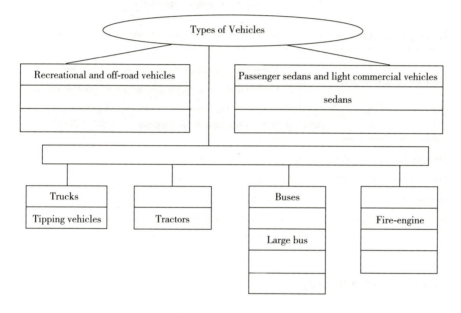

Lesson 2

Automobile Engine Ⅰ

Learning Objectives

Master the basic knowledge and skills	
➤ Language learning objective	Grasp the new words about the automobile engine.
➤ Skill learning objectives	1. Know the classification of the automobile engine. 2. Understand the components of the automobile engine.
Develop core competences of English	
➤ Be able to express different parts of an engine in English. ➤ Develop the positive attitude to overcome obstacles in English learning. ➤ Develop image recognition ability in workplace. ➤ Develop the abilities of self-assessment and self-improvement efficiently.	

Part One: Warming-up

Look at the pictures and then tell the type of each engine.

Fig. 2-1　Types of engines

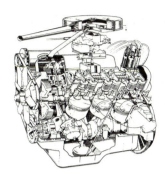

Fig. 2-1 Types of engines (cont.)

There are two main mechanisms in an automobile engine. One is crank-connecting rod mechanism, the other is valve train.

Part Two: Text

Automobile Engine I

The engine gives the **power** to the automobile. It can turn fuel into the **energy** of auto-power. And without the engine, the automobile will not be able to move, so the engine is usually called the "heart" of the automobile. The engine can be classified in the following ways:

1. Fuel type: **gasoline** engine, **diesel** engine, gas engine.
2. The number of **cylinders**: 2~12 cylinders.
3. **Arrangement** of cylinders: in line (3~5 cylinders), V-type (6, 8, 10, 12 cylinders); flat-horizontally opposed.
4. Cubic capacity/piston displacement: 1.5~5 litres.
5. **Valve train**/valve mechanism: OHV, OHC, SOHC and DOHC. Valve train consists of intake valve, exhaust **valve**, **camshaft**, valve oil seal, valve spring and valve lifter.
6. The number of **strokes** per cycle: Two-stroke or Four-stroke.
7. Method of **ignition**: spark or **compression**.
8. **Cooling** type: **air-cooled**, **liquid-cooled.**
9. **Turbocharging**: Some engines have a turbocharger. Turbocharging **enables** more air to be forced into the cylinders, and this can **increase** engine **performance**.

turn...into 把……变成
energy 能量
be classified 分类成
in the way 以……方式
gasoline 汽油
diesel 柴油
arrangement 排列
cubic capacity 容积
litre 升
ignition 点火
cooling 冷却
air-cooled 风冷
liquid-cooled 水冷
turbocharging 涡轮增压
enable 使……能够
be forced 被迫
increase 增加
performance 性能

Part Three: Words Study

power 做功，动力
cylinder 气缸
in line 直列式
V-tape V 型
valve train 配气机构
OHV 顶置气门
OHC 顶置凸轮轴
intake 进气
exhaust 排气

valve 气门，阀
camshaft 连杆
stroke 冲程
compression 压缩
piston 活塞
connecting rod 连杆
spark plug 火花塞
crankshaft 曲轴

Part Four: Knowledge Extension

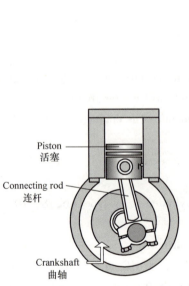

Fig. 2-2 The main components of the cylinder

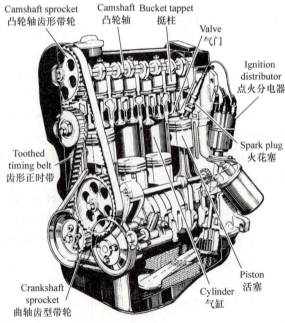

Fig. 2-3 Components of the engine

Module One Automobile English 汽车英语

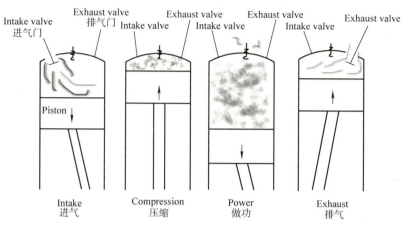

Fig. 2-4   4-stroke of an engine

Part Five: Practice

I. Translate our English names into Chinese.

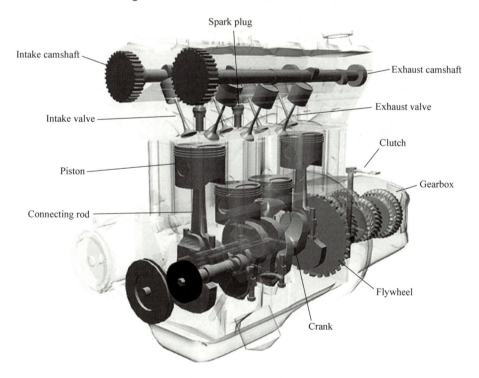

Fig. 2-5   Practice I

11

Ⅱ. Match the letters with the right terms.

A.

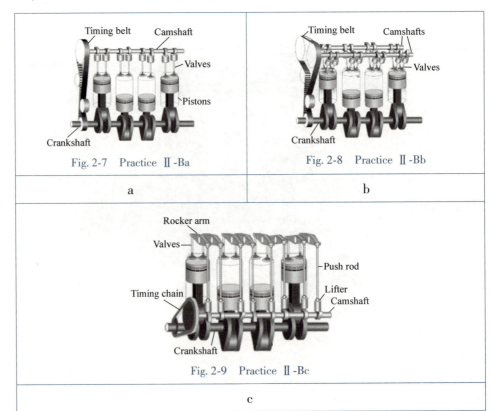

Fig. 2-6　Practice Ⅱ-A

crankshaft （　　　　　）
exhaust camshaft （　　　　　）
intake camshaft （　　　　　）
piston （　　　　　）
connecting rod （　　　　　）
spark plug （　　　　　）
left：exhaust valve （　　　　　）
right：intake valve （　　　　　）
cooling water ducts

B

4-cylinder 8-valve OHV engine （　　　）, 4-cylinder 8-valve SOHC engine （　　　）,
4-cylinder 16-valve DOHC engine （　　　）

a	b

Fig. 2-7　Practice Ⅱ-Ba　　Fig. 2-8　Practice Ⅱ-Bb

Fig. 2-9　Practice Ⅱ-Bc

c

Ⅲ. Order and state them.

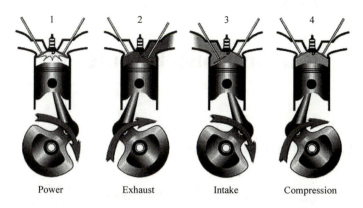

Fig. 2-10   Practice Ⅲ

Ⅳ. What are we? Write our English names.

Fig. 2-11   Practice Ⅳ

Lesson 3

Automobile Engine II

 Learning Objectives

Master the basic knowledge and skills	
➢ Language learning objective	Grasp the new words about automobile engine.
➢ Skill learning objectives	1. Understand the five systems of the engine and their components. 2. Know the functions of different systems.
Develop core competences of English	

➢ Be able to express different parts of each system in English.
➢ Develop the positive attitude to overcome obstacles in English learning.
➢ Develop image recognition ability in workplace.
➢ Develop the abilities of self-assessment and self-improvement efficiently.

Part One: Warming-up

Look at the pictures, what are these systems?

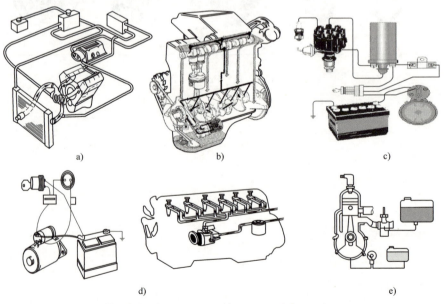

Fig. 3-1　Components and systems of the engine
Fuel system　lubrication system　starting system　ignition system　cooling system

Module One Automobile English 汽车英语

 There are five systems in an engine. They are fuel system, cooling system, lubrication system, ignition system and starting system.

Part Two: Text

Automobile Engine II

1. **Fuel system**—The **fuel system pumps gasoline** from the gasoline **tank** and **mixes** it with air so that the proper air-fuel **mixture** can flow into the cylinders.

2. **Lubrication system**—The lubrication system must ensure that every moving part in the engine can get oil so that they can move **easily**. The two main components needing oil are pistons and bearings, and they can make the components like the crankshaft and camshafts **rotate freely**.

3. **Cooling system**—The cooling system in most cars consists of the **radiator** and water pump. Water **circulates** through **passages** around the cylinders and then **travels** through the radiator to **cool** it **off**.

4. **Ignition system**—The **ignition system produces** a high-**voltage** electrical charge and **transmits** it to the spark plugs, to **ignite** the air-fuel mixture in the cylinders, which **initiate** the power stroke.

5. **Starting system**—A starter is an electric motor that starts the engine.

mix 混合
easily 容易地
allow 允许
rotate 旋转
freely 自如地
circulate 循环
passage 通道
travel 经过
cool...off 使……冷却
produce 产生
ignite 点火

Part Three: Words Study

fuel system 燃油系统	voltage 电压
pump 泵	transmit 传输
gasoline 汽油	initiate 起动,发动
tank 燃油箱	starting system 起动系统
mixture 混合物	injector 喷油器
lubrication system 润滑系统	oil pump 机油泵
cooling system 冷却系统	bearing 轴承
radiator 散热器	fan 风扇
ignition system 点火系统	

Part Four: Knowledge Extension

1. Fuel system

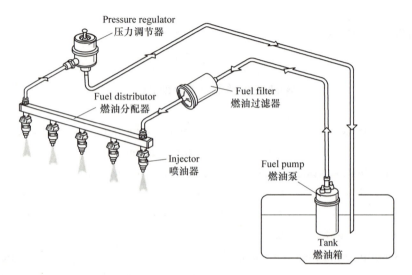

Fig. 3-2　Components of the fuel system

2. Lubrication system

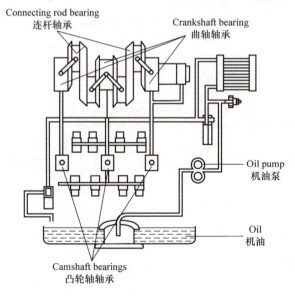

Fig. 3-3　Components of the lubrication system

3. Cooling system

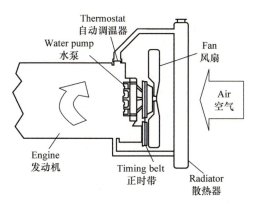

Fig. 3-4 Components of the cooling system

Part Five: Practice

Ⅰ. Translate English into Chinese.

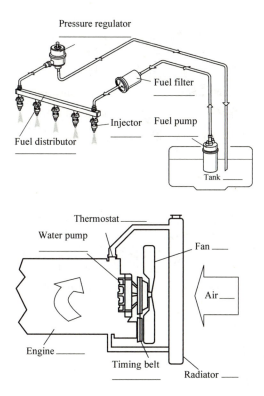

Fig. 3-5 Practice Ⅰ

II. Translate Chinese into English.

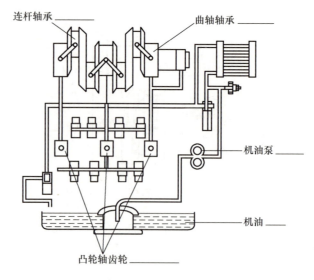

Fig. 3-6　Practice II

III. Match the letters in each car with the right terms.

A.

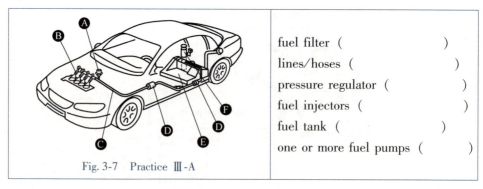

Fig. 3-7　Practice III-A

fuel filter (　　　　　　)

lines/hoses (　　　　　　)

pressure regulator (　　　　　　)

fuel injectors (　　　　　　)

fuel tank (　　　　　　)

one or more fuel pumps (　　　　　　)

B.

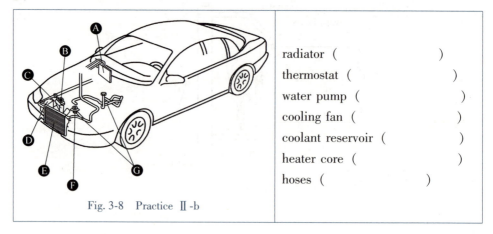

Fig. 3-8　Practice II-b

radiator (　　　　　　)

thermostat (　　　　　　)

water pump (　　　　　　)

cooling fan (　　　　　　)

coolant reservoir (　　　　　　)

heater core (　　　　　　)

hoses (　　　　　　)

Ⅳ. What are we? Write out the systems of the engine.

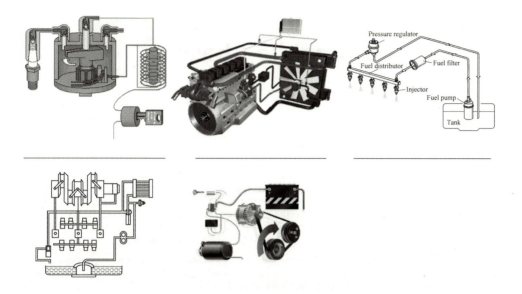

_____   _____   _____

_____   _____

Fig. 3-9　Practice Ⅳ

Ⅴ. Write out two or three key components in each system.

1. Fuel system _____
2. Lubrication system _____
3. Cooling system _____

 Lesson 4

Automobile Chassis Ⅰ

Learning Objectives

Master the basic knowledge and skills	
➢ Language learning objective	Grasp the new words about automobile chassis.
➢ Skill learning objectives	1. Understand the structure of the chassis. 2. Know the functions of the front and rear suspension.
Develop core competences of English	
➢ Be able to express different parts of the suspension in English. ➢ Develop the positive attitude to overcome obstacles in English learning. ➢ Develop image recognition ability in workplace. ➢ Develop the abilities of self-assessment and self-improvement efficiently.	

Part One: Warming-up

Look at the picture and guess their Chinese names.

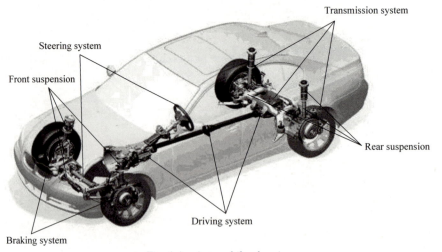

Fig. 4-1 Automobile chassis

Module One Automobile English 汽车英语

I'm automobile chassis. I'm made up of car frame, springs, shock absorbers, driving shaft, brakes, tires and wheels.

Part Two: Text

Automobile Chassis

The **chassis** is the under **portion** of an automobile. It consists of the **transmission** system, **driving** system, **steering** system and **braking** system. The chassis has three major functions: 1) to **support** and install the car body, engine and other major parts; 2) to receive and transmit the power of the engine; 3) to **ensure** the normal running of the vehicle. The main components of the chassis are **suspension**, **frame**, **springs**, **shock absorbers**, **driving shaft**, **brakes**, **tires** and **wheels** and so on.

There are two major parts for suspension.

1. Front suspension

The front suspension allows the front wheels to move up and down, and absorb road shocks. And it also allows the front wheels to swing from side to side so that the car can be steered.

2. Rear suspension

The rear suspension uses **leaf springs**, **arranged** at one wheel. The leaf spring is **anchored** at three places: the **front hanger**, the **rear shackle** and the **axle housing**.

portion 部分
transmission 传动
drive 行驶
steer 转向
brake 制动
support 支撑
suspension 悬架
ensure 确保
driving shaft 传动轴
brake 制动器
tire 轮胎
wheel 车轮
arrangement 排列
anchor 安装，固定
front hanger 前支架
rear shackle 后吊耳
axle housing 桥壳

Part Three: Words Study

chassis 底盘
transmission system 传动系统
driving system 行驶系统
steering system 转向系统
braking system 制动系统
shock absorber 减振器
frame 车架
spring 弹簧

front suspension 前悬架
rear suspension 后悬架
hanger 支架
coil spring 螺旋弹簧
leaf spring 钢板弹簧
lower control arm 下控制臂
trailing arm 纵臂
stub axle 销轴

Part Four: Knowledge Extension

1. Front suspension

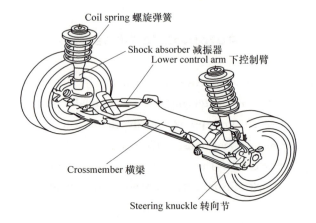

Fig. 4-2 Components of the front suspension

2. Rear suspension

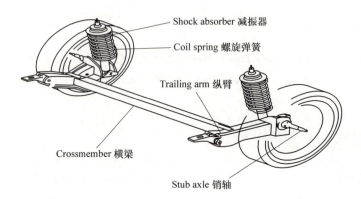

Fig. 4-3 Components of the rear suspension

Module One Automobile English 汽车英语

Part Five: Practice

Ⅰ. Write out our Chinese or English names.

A.

B.

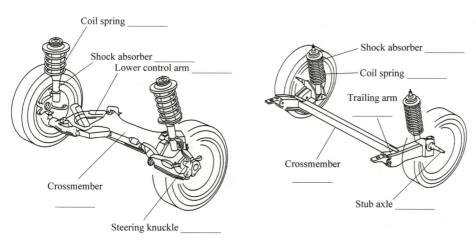

Fig. 4-4   Practice Ⅰ-A

Fig. 4-5   Practice Ⅰ-B

C.

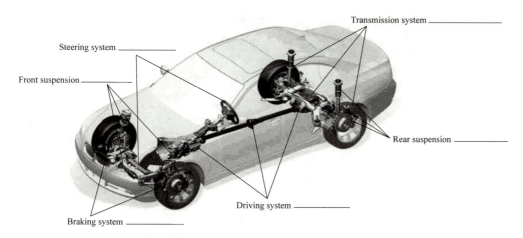

Fig. 4-6   Practice Ⅰ-C

Ⅱ. Judge the front and rear suspension and write out the English name.

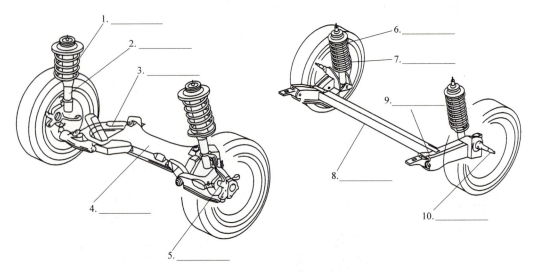

Fig. 4-7   Practice Ⅱ

Ⅲ. Write out the English name.

Fig. 4-8   Practice Ⅲ

Ⅳ. Find out the words.

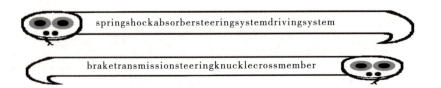

Module One Automobile English 汽车英语

Ⅴ. Fill in the blanks.

1. Write out the four systems of the chassis:
_____, _____, _____, _____
2. Write out the three functions of the chassis:
1) _____
2) _____
3) _____

Lesson 5

Automobile Chassis Ⅱ

Learning Objectives

Master the basic knowledge and skills	
➢ Language learning objective	Grasp the new words about the four systems of the chassis.
➢ Skill learning objectives	1. Know the functions of different systems. 2. Grasp the key components of each system.
Develop core competences of English	

➢ Develop the ability to search for information about the automobile chassis on the Internet.
➢ Develop the positive attitude to overcome obstacles in English learning.
➢ Develop image recognition ability in workplace.
➢ Develop the abilities of self-assessment and self-improvement efficiently.

Part One: Warming-up

Look at the picture and guess their Chinese names.

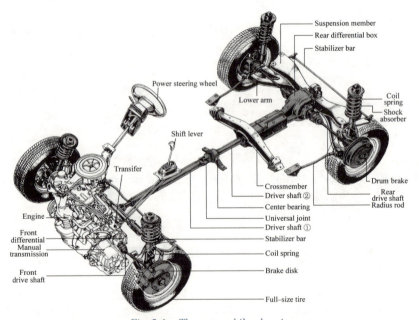

Fig. 5-1 The automobile chassis

Engine 发动机　Front differential 前差速器　Manual transmission 手动变速器　Front shaft 前半轴
Power steering wheel 动力转向盘　Shift lever 变速杆　Crossmember 横梁　Driver shaft 传动轴
Center bearing 中间轴承　Universal joint 万向节　Stabilizer bar 稳定杆　Coil spring 螺旋弹簧
Brake disk 制动盘　Full-size tire 全尺寸轮胎　Suspension member 悬架总成　Rear differential box 后差速器箱
Shock absorber 减振器　Drum brake 制动鼓　Rear shaft 后半轴　Radius rod 纵向推力杆

Module One　Automobile English 汽车英语

I'm automobile chassis and I have four main systems: transmission system, driving system, steering system and braking system.

Part Two: Text

Four Systems of the Chassis

1. Transmission system

The transmission system can transmit the power of the engine to the wheel and ensure the vehicle drive normally under all conditions. The main components of the transmission system are **clutch**, **transmission**, **driving shaft**, **main speed reducer**, **differential**, **universal joint**, **half axle** and **driving shaft**.

2. Driving system

The driving system has three basic **functions**: to receive power from driving shaft, to support **gross weight** of the vehicle and to **ease** the **impact** on car body caused by **uneven** roads, so as to provide a comfortable **driving environment** for the passengers. The main components of the driving system are **frame**, **axle**, **suspension**, **tires** and **wheels**.

3. Steering system

The steering system is a steering control and steering transmission **mechanism**. The main components of the steering system are **steering wheel**, **steering gear**, **steering shaft**, **steering shock absorber**, **steering tie rod** and **steering arm**.

4. Braking system

The braking system is to make a moving car slow down or stop as **requested** by drivers. The main components of the braking system are **brake pedal**, **brake disks**, **brake drums**, **brake master cylinder** and **brake valve**.

main speed reducer 主减速器
function 功能
gross 总的
weight 质量
ease 减轻
impact 冲击
uneven 不平的
driving environment 乘车环境
mechanism 机械装置
steering shock absorber 转向减振器
request 要求
brake master cylinder 制动总泵

Part Three: Words Study

tire 轮胎
clutch 离合器
transmission 变速器
driving shaft 传动轴
differential 差速器
universal joint 万向节
half axle 半轴
drive axle 驱动桥
driving shaft 驱动轴
wheel 车轮
main speed reducer 主减速器

steering wheel 转向盘
steering gear 转向器
steering shaft 转向轴
steering tie rod 转向横拉杆
steering arm 转向臂
brake drum 制动鼓
brake booster 制动助力器
brake valve 制动阀
brake disk 制动盘
brake master cylinder 制动总泵
brake pedal 制动踏板

Part Four: Knowledge Extension

Ⅰ. Transmission system

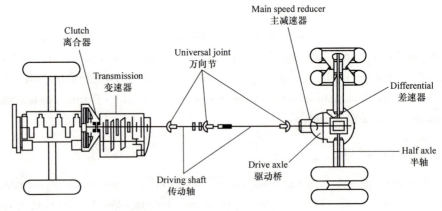

Fig. 5-2　Structure of the transmission system

Ⅱ. Driving system

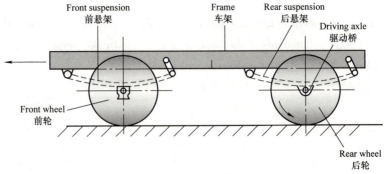

Fig. 5-3　Structure of the driving system

Module One   Automobile English 汽车英语

III. Braking system

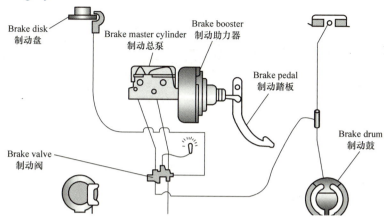

Fig. 5-4 Structure of the braking system

IV. Steering system

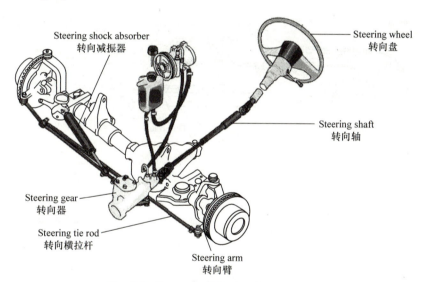

Fig. 5-5 Structure of the steering system

Part Five: Practice

I. Write out our Chinese and English names.

Fig. 5-6 Practice I

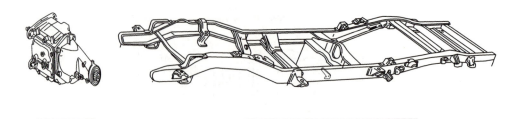

Fig. 5-6　Practice Ⅰ（cont.）

Ⅱ. Translate English into Chinese.

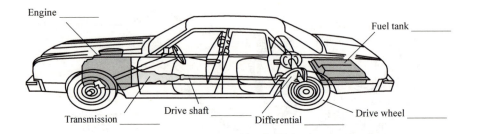

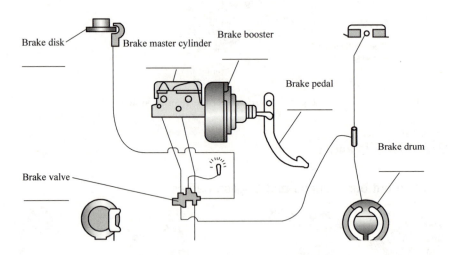

Fig. 5-7　Practice Ⅱ

Ⅲ. Classify the following words.

> brake pedal, steering wheel, differential, frame, driving axle, tires, brake drums, shock absorber, spring, clutch, steering gear, steering tie rod, drive axle, steering gear, wheel, steering arm, brake disk, driving shaft, transmission, suspension, steering shaft, brake valve, half axle, universal joint

1. Transmission system: _____
2. Driving system: _____
3. Steering system: _____
4. Braking system: _____

 Lesson 6

Automobile Electrical System Ⅰ

Learning Objectives

Master the basic knowledge and skills	
➤ Language learning objective	Grasp the new words about automobile electrical system.
➤ Skill learning objectives	1. Know the different parts of automobile electrical system. 2. Grasp the definition of electrical system.
Develop core competences of English	

➤ Develop the ability to search for information about the automobile chassis on the Internet.
➤ Develop the positive attitude to overcome obstacles in English learning.
➤ Develop image recognition ability in workplace.
➤ Develop the abilities of self-assessment and self-improvement efficiently.

Part One: Warming-up

Look at the picture and guess their Chinese names.

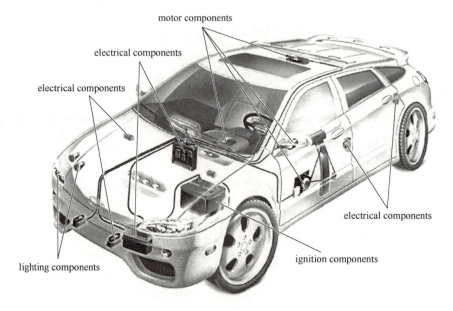

Fig. 6-1 Components of the electrical system (1)

> I'm the electrical system. I can produce, store and distribute all the electrical parts that auto requires. So do you want to know the composition of me? Please read the article below.

Part Two: Text

The composition of the electrical system

The electrical system is an important part of the vehicle, and its performance affects the power, **economy**, **reliability**, safety, comfort of the vehicle. Its **technological content** has become one of the important indicators for measuring the grade of modern vehicles. The electrical system of modern vehicles can be divided into the following four parts according to its purpose:

1. The **charging system** is made up of batteries, alternators, and voltage regulators. It is used to charge the battery and to provide power for electronic components and other **electronic** systems.

2. The **electricity system** includes starting system, ignition system, instrument system, **lighting and signal system**, electronic control system and **auxiliary electrical appliances**.

3. The **detection system** includes various detection instruments and various warning lights to detect the working conditions of the engine and other devices.

4. The **power distribution system** includes a **central junction box**, **circuit switches**, safety devices, wires, etc. It can ensure the reliability and safety of the circuit work.

In addition, electric vehicles contain **power batteries management system**, motor drive system and vehicle control system instead of engine and gearbox.

economy 经济性
technological content 科技含量
be divided into 被分成
according to 根据
be made up of 由……组成
be used to 被用作……
lighting and signal system 照明与信号系统
circuit switches 电路开关
power batteries management system 动力电池管理系统

Part Three: Words Study

reliability 可靠性
charging system 电源系统
electricity system 用电系统
auxiliary electrical appliances 辅助电器
detection system 检测系统
power distribution system 配电系统
central junction box 中央接线盒

relay 继电器
battery 电池
fuse 保险
alternator 交流发电机
regulator 调节器
ignition coil 点火线圈
ECU 电子控制装置
fusible link 易熔线

Part Four: Knowledge Extension

1. The structure of Electrical system

A

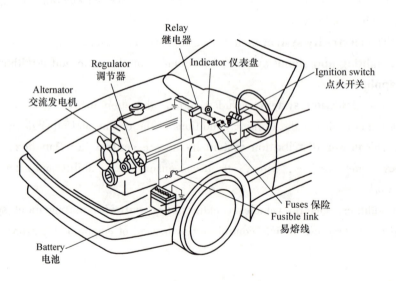

Fig. 6-2　Components of the electrical system（2）

Module One Automobile English 汽车英语

B

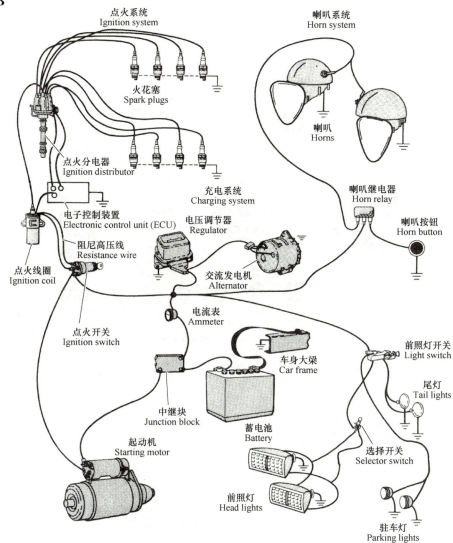

Fig. 6-3　Components of the electrical system（3）

2. The structure of charging system

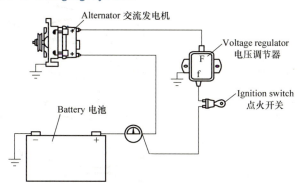

Fig. 6-4　Components of charging system

35

3. The power distribution system

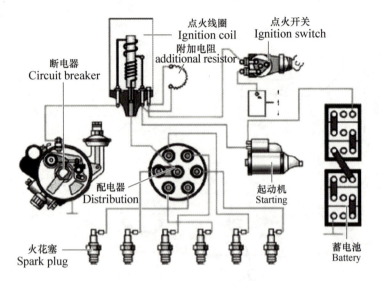

Fig. 6-5 The power distribution system

Part Five: Practice

Ⅰ. Write out the components of the following systems.

（1）The charging system

（2）The electricity system

（3）The detection system

（4）The power distribution system

II. Translate English into Chinese.

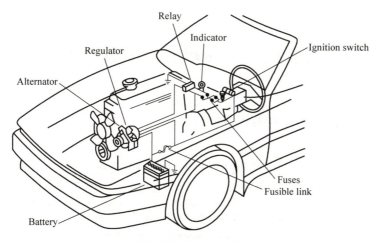

Fig. 6-6　Practice II

regulator _____　　　relay _____　　　indicator _____
alternator _____　　　fuse _____　　　fusible link _____
Ignition switch _____　　　battery _____

III. Words Puzzle.

Alt__rn__tor　　　　　r_l_y　　　　　f____e
distri__utor　　　　　ci__cuit　　　　a__met__r
sw__tch　　　　　　　re__ulator　　　fu__ible
i__nition　　　　　　be__t　　　　　c__mponent

IV. Search for the information on the Internet then write down the English and Chinese names of the structure of the ignition system.

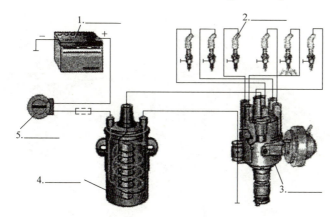

Fig. 6-7　Practice IV

1. _____　2. _____　3. _____　4. _____　5. _____

Lesson 7

Automobile Electrical System Ⅱ

Learning Objectives

Master the basic knowledge and skills	
➢ Language learning objective	Grasp the new words about the electricity system.
➢ Skill learning objectives	1. Understand the classification of electricity system. 2. Know the functions of ignition system and starting system.
Develop core competences of English	

➢ Develop the ability to search for information about the electricity system on the Internet.
➢ Develop the positive attitude to overcome obstacles in English learning.
➢ Develop image recognition ability in workplace.
➢ Develop the abilities of self-assessment and self-improvement efficiently.

Part One: Warming-up

Look at the picture and guess their Chinese names.

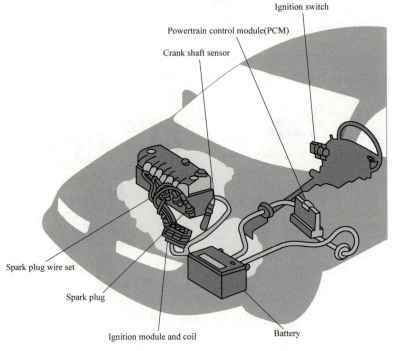

Fig. 7-1 Major components of ignition system

Module One Automobile English 汽车英语

Do you know the composition of ignition system and starting system. Can you guess the major parts of them? Here are some brief introduction of ignition and starting system.

Part Two: Text

Classification of the electricity system

The electricity system is an very important part of electrical system. It mainly contains ignition system, **starting system** and instrument system, etc.

All **gasoline engines** need **some form** of ignition system. This system is made up of the battery, **ignition switch**, distributor, condenser ignition coil, spark plugs, resistor, low and high voltage wires.

It has two **functions**: one is to <u>step up</u> the battery from the low voltage to the high voltage, and the other is to **control** the ignition **timing** to meet the needs of the engine. It also has two circuits: the <u>primary circuit</u> and the <u>secondary circuit</u>.

The starting system is the heart of the electrical system. It provides the power to start the engine. It is made up of the battery, starting switch, starter relay and starting **motor**.

<u>Besides</u>, there are still other systems. They are the **lighting system**, **horn system** and air-conditioning system. They have close relation to the electricity system.

gasoline engine
汽油发动机
some form 某种形式
function 功能
step up 升高
control 控制
timing 正时
primary circuit 初级电路
secondary circuit 次级电路
besides 此外

Part Three: Words Study

starting system 起动系统	driving belt 传动带
ignition switch 点火开关	flywheel 飞轮
condenser 电容器	starting motor 起动
spark plug 火花塞	ECM 电子控制模块
starting motor 起动机	main fuse 主熔断线
lighting system 照明系统	voltage regulator 电压调节器
horn system 喇叭系统	

Part Four: Knowledge Extension

1. The major components of the starting system

A

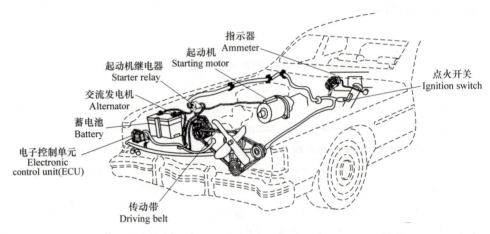

Fig. 7-2　Starting system

B

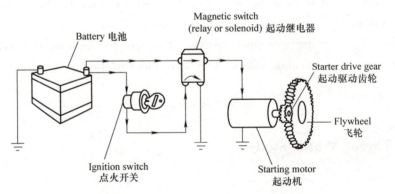

Fig. 7-3　Components of starting system

2. The structure of the ignition system

A.

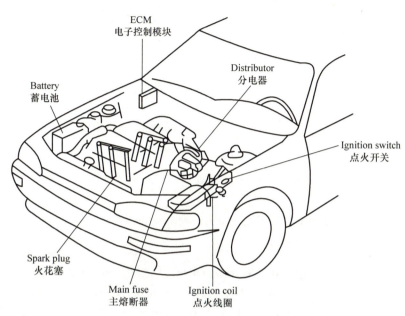

Fig. 7-4　Major components of the ignition system

B.

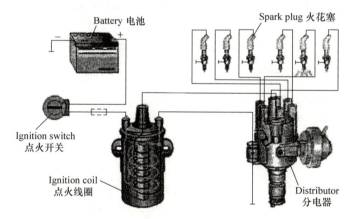

Fig. 7-5　Structure of the ignition system

Part Five：Practice

Ⅰ．Match column A with column B.

A.

1. starter drive gear （　　　）
2. alternator （　　　）

B.

A. 启动驱动齿轮
B. 交流发电机

3. voltage regulator （　　　）　C. 传动带
4. driving belt （　　　）　D. 电压调节器
5. starting motor （　　　）　E. 飞轮
6. flywheel （　　　）　F. 起动机

Ⅱ. Translate English into Chinese.

1. starting system_____　　5. ECM_____
2. lighting system_____　　6. ignition switch_____
3. horn system_____　　7. magnetic switch_____
4. main fuse_____　　8. spark plug_____

Ⅲ. Fill in the blanks with the words and phrases in the box.

> starter driver gear, starting switch, starting motor,
> lighting system, battery

1. _____ is to provide electrical energy （电能） to operate the starter.
2. _____ is to open and close the circuit between the battery and starter.
3. _____ is to transmit （传输） the starter's rotation （起动机旋转） to the flywheel of the engine.
4. _____ includes the external lights, internal lights （车外灯） and signal light （信号灯）.
5. _____ is to convert electrical energy （电能） to mechanical energy （机械能） to run the engine.

Ⅳ. Translation English into Chinese.

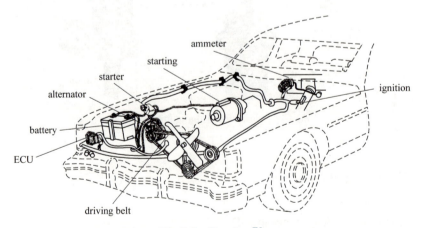

Fig. 7-6　Practice Ⅳ

Module One Automobile English 汽车英语

Lesson 8

Automobile Body

Learning Objectives

Master the basic knowledge and skills	
➢ Language learning objective	Grasp the new words about the automobile body.
➢ Skill learning objectives	1. Understand the structure of the automobile body. 2. Know seven basic body shapes used today.
Develop core competences of English	

➢ Develop the ability to search for information about automobile body on the Internet.
➢ Develop the positive attitude to overcome obstacles in English learning.
➢ Develop image recognition ability in workplace.
➢ Develop the abilities of self-assessment and self-improvement efficiently.

Part One: Warming-up

Look at the picture and guess their Chinese names.

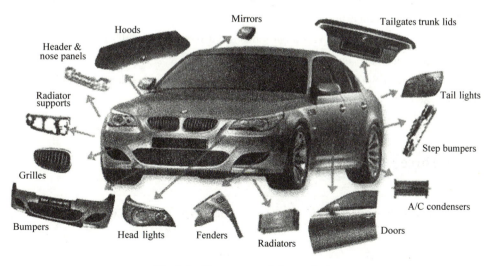

Fig. 8-1 Components of the car body

43

I'm the body of the automobile, including windows, doors, a hood, a roof, the instrument panel, speedometer, car radio, seats, lamps, etc. inside.

Part Two: Text

Automobile Body

The body is the place where the driver works and passengers or goods are **contained.** It includes a hood, doors, tailgates, mirrors, fenders, grilles, headlights and taillights. It **provides** a **protective covering** for the engine, passengers and goods.

There are seven **basic** body **shapes** used today.

1. Body of a sedan: A vehicle with front and back seats can **hold** four to six people. Either a two or four doors **design** can be **available** for the sedan.

2. Body of a **convertible**: Convertibles have **vinyl** roof that can **be raised or lowered.**

3. Body of a life back or a hatchback: The **distinguishing feature** of this vehicle is its rear **luggage compartment**, which has more space for the passengers.

4. Body of a station wagon: A **station wagon** is **characterized** by its roof. It **extends** straight back and has a bigger interior luggage compartment in the rear.

5. Body of a pickup vehicle: Pickup vehicle's body has an open **cargo** area behind the driver's compartment.

6. Body of a van: The **van's** body has a tall roof and a totally enclosed can load large cargo, and have enough space.

7. Body of a Sport Utility Vehicle (SUV): This classification of vehicle covers **a range of** body designs.

contain 包含
provide 提供
protective 保护的
covering 遮盖物
basic 基本的
shape 形状
hold 容纳
design 设计
available 可得到的
convertible 敞篷汽车
vinyl 乙烯树脂
be raised/lowered 升、降
distinguishing 显著的
feature 特征
luggage 行李
compartment 分隔间,箱室
station wagon 旅行车
characterize 表现……特性
extend 伸展
cargo 货物
van 货柜车
a range of 很多的

Part Three: Words Study

hood 发动机罩
fender 翼子板
trunk lid 行李舱盖
bumper 保险杠

rear view mirror 后视镜
sun visor 遮阳板
seat 座椅
head restraint 安全头枕

door lock switch 门锁
grill 通气栏
window 车窗
roof 顶篷
carpet 脚垫

speaker 喇叭
room lamp 顶灯
seat belt 安全带
arm rest 臂枕
map lamp 阅读灯

Part Four: Knowledge Extension

I. The outside of a car

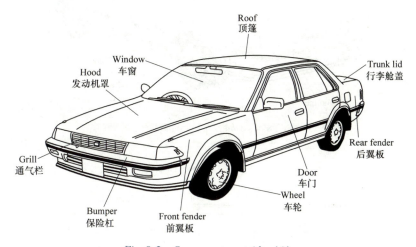

Fig. 8-2　Components outside（1）

II. The inside of a car

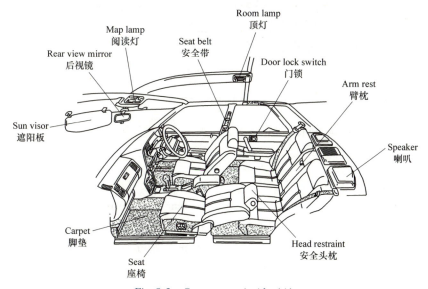

Fig. 8-3　Components inside（1）

Part Five: Practice

Ⅰ. Translate English into Chinese.

A.

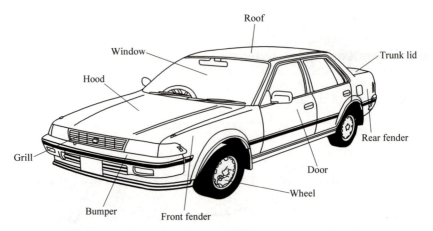

Fig. 8-4 Components outside (2)

B.

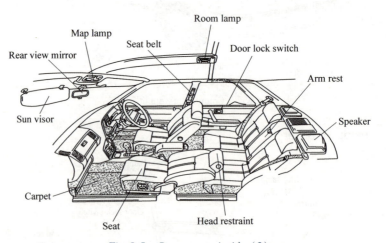

Fig. 8-5 Components inside (2)

Ⅱ. Match column A with column B.

A	B
1. 后视镜（　　）	a. speaker
2. 臂枕（　　）	b. rear view mirror
3. 遮阳板（　　）	c. head restraint
4. 安全带（　　）	d. map lamp
5. 顶灯（　　）	e. carpet
6. 座椅（　　）	f. door lock switch

Module One Automobile English 汽车英语

7. 阅读灯（　　　）　　　　g. arm rest
8. 脚垫（　　　）　　　　　h. seat belt
9. 安全头枕（　　　）　　　i. seat
10. 门锁（　　　）　　　　 j. room lamp
11. 喇叭（　　　）　　　　 k. sun visor

Ⅲ. Find out the words.

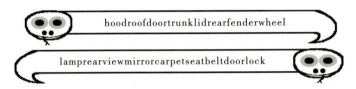

hoodroofdoortrunklidrearfenderwheel

lamprearviewmirrorcarpetseatbeltdoorlock

Ⅳ. Words puzzle.

re _ r-f _ nd _ r   tr _ nk-l _ d   m _ rr _ r
c _ _ p _ t   h _ _ d   wh _ _ l
l _ mp   s _ _ t   l _ ck
w _ nd _ w

 Lesson 9

Fuel Economy

Learning Objectives

Master the basic knowledge and skills	
➢ Language learning objective	Grasp the new words about the fuel economy.
➢ Skill learning objectives	1. Understand the definition of the fuel economy. 2. Know the definition of Constant Speed Fuel Consumption and Road Cycle Fuel Consumption.
Develop the core literacy of English subject	

➢ Develop the ability to search for information about the fuel economy on the Internet.
➢ Develop the positive attitude to overcome obstacles in English learning.
➢ Develop image recognition ability in workplace.
➢ Develop the abilities of self-assessment and self-improvement efficiently.

Part One: Warming-up

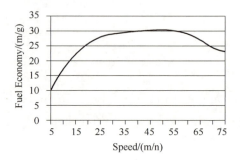

Fig. 9-1 Fuel economy

 I'm the fuel economy of a car. I'm the distance travelled per unit volume of fuel used: kilometers per litre (km/L) or miles per gallon (MPG).

Module One Automobile English 汽车英语

Part Two: Text

Fuel Economy

The **fuel economy** of a car refers to the distance travelled per unit **volume** of fuel used. It can be **measured** by kilometers per **litre** (km/L) or **miles per gallon** (**MPG**). **Fuel consumption** is an important index to measure the fuel economy of a car. It is the the amount of fuel consumed per unit distance, for instance, litres per 100 kilometers (L/100km). It includes constant speed fuel consumption and road cycle fuel consumption.

CSFC (**Constant Speed Fuel Consumption**): it refers to the fuel economy index of a car when driving at a constant speed under good road conditions. Due to various operating conditions such as **acceleration**, **deceleration**, **braking**, and **engine idling**, the car often has low fuel consumption at constant speed, which is quite different from the actual fuel consumption.

Road Cycle Fuel Consumption: It is the fuel economy index measured when the car is **repeatedly cycled** on the road at **prescribed** speed in **stipulated** time. It is also called multi-condition road cycle fuel consumption.

refer to 涉及
per unit 每段距离
the amount of ……的数量

repeatedly 重复地
prescribe 规定
stipulated 规定的

Part Three: Words Study

fuel economy 燃油经济
volume 总量
measure 测量，估量
litre 升
MPG (miles per gallon) 每加仑汽油行驶的英里数
fuel consumption 油耗
acceleration 加速
CSFC (Constant Speed Fuel consumption) 等速油耗
deceleration 减速
brake 制动
engine idling 发动机怠速
Road Cycle Fuel Consumption 道路循环油耗
cycle 循环
MPH (miles per hour) 英里每小时

49

Part Four: Knowledge Extension

1. Comparison table of fuel consumption of some models.

Model 车型	Displacement 排量/L	Gearbox 变速器	City fuel consumption 城市油耗 (L/100km)	Suburban fuel consumption 郊区油耗 (L/100km)
Toyota Camry	2.0	Automatic transmission	8.6	5.4
Honda Accord	1.5T	CVT	7.6	5.1
Magotan	2.0T	Double clutch	8.2	5.1
Passat	2.0T	Double clutch	9.5	5.6
Teana	2.5	CVT	10.4	5.8
Regal	2.0T	Automatic transmission	10.1	5.8
Audi A4	2.0T	Double clutch	7.5	5
BMW3	2.0T	Automatic transmission	8	5.3
Mercedes-Benz C200	2.0T	Automatic transmission	8.1	5.2
Cadillac XTS	2.0T	Automatic transmission	10.7	6.3

Fig. 9-2 Comparison table of fuel consumption of some models

2. Midsize passenger car fuel economy.

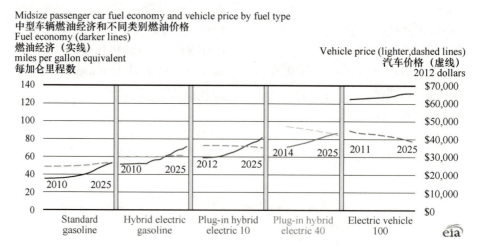

Fig. 9-3 Midsize passenger car fuel economy

Module One Automobile English 汽车英语

Part Five: Practice

I. Translate the following expressions into English.

耗油量 _____   发动机怠速 _____
燃油经济性 _____   每加仑汽油行驶的英里数 _____
等速油耗 _____   英里每小时 _____
循环油耗 _____   加速 _____

II. Words puzzle.

con__um__tion   fu__l   c__cl__
me__sur__   cons__me   l__tre
sp____d   v__hicl__   am____nt

III. Fill in the blanks with the words and phrases in the box.

fuel economy, acceleration, fuel consumption, litre, mile, volume, refer to

1. Anything that is listed as less than 6-litres/100km or more than 16.5km/1-litre is considered to be a pretty _____ .
2. The capacity of this storage tank is 10 _____ .
3. _____ to 60 mph takes a mere 5.7 seconds.
4. _____ is the amount of fuel consumed in driving a given distance.
5. The distance travelled per unit _____ of fuel used is so much.
6. CSFC _____ the fuel economy index of a car when driving at a constant speed under good road conditions.
7. The car consumes 7L gasoline per 100 _____ .

IV. Answer the following questions.

1. What is the definition of "Constant-Speed Fuel Consumption"?
   _____
2. What is the definition of "Road Cycle Fuel Consumption"?
   _____
3. What are the factors that affect the fuel consumption of automobiles?
   _____

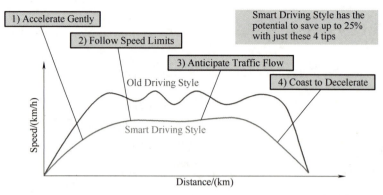

Fig. 9-4　Practice Ⅳ

① Design and manufacture of automobiles: such as engine displacement, engine design, gear box, body weight, shape design, etc.

② Personal driving habits;

③ Traffic

④ Oil quality

⑤ Weather

Module One Automobile English 汽车英语

Lesson 10

Automobile Safety, Comfortable Equipment and Maneuverability

Learning Objectives

Master the basic knowledge and skills	
➢ Language learning objective	Grasp the new words about automobile performance.
➢ Skill learning objectives	1. Know the specific manifestations of automobile safety. 2. Understand the influencing factors of automobile comfortable. 3. Understand the determinants of automobile handling.
Develop the core literacy of English subject	

➢ Develop the ability to search for information about safety equipment on the Internet.
➢ Develop the positive attitude to overcome obstacles in English learning.
➢ Develop image recognition ability in workplace.
➢ Develop the abilities of self-assessment and self-improvement efficiently.

Part One: Warming-up

Look at the pictures and guess what these safety features are.

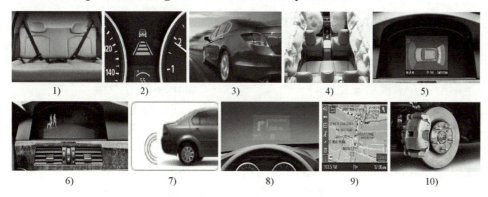

Fig. 10-1 Safety equipments of a vehicle

1) Seat Belts 安全带 2) Active Cruise Control 定速巡航控制 3) Vehicle Stability Assist 车身稳定辅助装置 4) Front, Front Side and Side Curtain Airbags 前窗、前侧及侧窗帘安全气囊 5) Park Distance Control 停车距离控制系统 6) Night Vision 夜间视野显示 7) Reverse Parking Sensors 倒车感应器 8) Head-Up Display HUD 抬头数字显示 9) Navigation System with RTTI 驾驶指南导航系统 10) 4-wheel Disc Brakes with Anti-lock Braking System (ABS) and Electronic Brake-force Distribution (EBD) 带防抱死制动系统及电子制动力分配系统的四轮制动盘

Various kinds of safety equipments keep the occupants away from danger, especially in an emergency.

Part Two: Text

Automobile Safety, Comfortable Equipment and Maneuverability

indispensable 不可缺少的
Accident 意外
injured 受伤的
prevent... from
预防，阻止

Automobile safety is an **indispensable** part of a vehicle. It can be divided into **active safety** and **passive safety**. Active safety **configuration** is a safety setting to prevent **accidents** in vehicles, such as **ABS**, **EBD**, **ESP**, etc. Therefore, active safety configuration is more important. Passive safety configuration is a safety setting that prevents people in the car from being injured after an accident, such as **airbags**.

The **indicators** of **comfort** include interior noise, the size of the interior space, the **filterability** of the suspension, the **supportability**, material and function of the seat, the **comfort** and smoothness of the gearbox, etc.

be determined by
由……决定
the guarantee of
……的保证

The handling of the vehicle is mainly determined by three factors: power, suspension and **steering system**. Power is the foundation of **maneuverability**, suspension is the key to maneuverability, and the steering system is the guarantee of maneuverability.

Part Three: Words and Phrases

active safety 主动安全
passive safety 被动安全
configuration 配置，结构
ABS (Anti-lock Braking System) 防抱死系统
EBD (Electronic Brake-force Distribution) 电子制动力分配系统
ESP (Electronic Stability Program) 车身电子稳定系统
SRS (Supplemental Restrain System) 辅助约束系统
airbags 安全气囊
indicator 指标，标志
comfort 舒适性
filterability 过滤性
suspension 悬架
supportability 支撑性
steering system 转向系统
maneuverability 可操作性

54

Module One   Automobile English 汽车英语

Part Four: Knowledge Extension

Fig. 10-2

Air bags as known as supplemental restrain system (SRS)——provides additional protection.

Fig. 10-3

Anti-lock Braking System (ABS)——helps prevent the wheels from locking up.

Fig. 10-4

Electronic Brake-force Distribution (EBD)——balances braking forces at each wheel.

Fig. 10-5

The adjustable seats——make driver and passengers feel more comfortable.

Fig. 10-6

Automatic transmission——make driving not so difficult.

Fig. 10-7

The steering wheel-mounted controls for cruise and audio system——makes driving more simple, and playing CD more effortless.

Fig. 10-8

The power windows——makes lift a little easier.

Fig. 10-9

The remote key——open the door without using the key.

Fig. 10-10

The air conditioning (空调) with air filtration system (空气过滤系统)——ensures that the temperature in the cabin is automatically held constant and the air quality is always fresh.

Fig. 10-11

Bluetooth Hands Free Link (蓝牙免提系统)——makes hands-free phone calls with your compatible phone simply by using the multi-function steering wheel controls and radio key.

Module One Automobile English 汽车英语

Part Five: Practice

I. Translate the following expressions into English.

主动安全配置 _____　　气囊 _____
被动安全配置 _____　　悬架 _____
转向系统 _____　　　　噪声 _____
防抱死系统 _____　　　电子制动力分配系统 _____
安全气囊 _____　　　　辅助约束系统 _____

II. Words puzzle.

con__iguration　　　　ind__ca__or　　　　st__ble
safet__　　　　　　　　co__fo__t　　　　　ma__euv__rability
sm__thn__ss　　　　　　h__ndle　　　　　　__ndisp__nsable

III. Look at pictures and write out their English names.

_____　　_____　　_____

_____　　_____　　_____

_____　　_____　　_____

Ⅳ. Answer the following questions.

1. What is "active safety configuration"?
_____

2. What is "passive safety configuration"?
_____

Ⅴ. Match column A with column B.

A	B
( ) Seat Belts	A. 倒车感应器
( ) Active Cruise Control	B. 夜间视野显示
( ) Navigation System with RTTI	C. 抬头数字显示
( ) Night Vision	D. 安全带
( ) Head-Up Display	E. 定速巡航控制
( ) EBD	F. 防抱死制动系统
( ) ABS	G. 电子制动力分配系统
( ) Reverse Parking Sensors	H. 驾驶指南导航系统

 Module One Automobile English 汽车英语

 Lesson 11

New Energy Vehicles

Learning Objectives

Master the basic knowledge and skills	
➤ Language learning objective	Grasp the new words about new energy vehicles.
➤ Skill learning objectives	1. Know the characteristic of new energy vehicles. 2. Understand the basic structure of new energy vehicles.
Develop the core literacy of English subject	

➤ Develop the ability to search for information about new energy vehicles on the Internet.
➤ Develop the positive attitude to overcome obstacles in English learning.
➤ Develop image recognition ability in workplace.
➤ Develop the abilities of self-assessment and self-improvement efficiently.

Part One: Warming-up

Biofuels

Electrical energy

Solar energy

Fig. 11-1 Automobile new energy

BYD Qin Endurance 300km

Fig. 11-2

Geely Emperor GSe Endurance 353~460km

Fig. 11-3

BAIC EU400 Endurance 260~460km

Fig. 11-4

Tesla Model X Endurance 355~565km

Fig. 11-5

Volkswagen Golf Endurance 255km

Fig. 11-6

Nissan Sylphy Endurance 338km

Fig. 11-7

 New energy vehicles are very popular nowadays. They use energy such as fuel cell, solar energy instead of gasoline and diesel.

Part Two: Text

New energy vehicles

New energy vehicles refer to all other energy vehicles except gasoline and diesel engines, including **fuel cell vehicles**, **hybrid vehicles**, **hydrogen powered vehicles**, and solar vehicles.

The **composition** of electric vehicles include electric drive and control systems, driving force transmission and other mechanical systems, and working devices that complete **predetermined** tasks. The electric drive and control system is the core of the electric vehicle. It <u>is composed of</u> the drive motor, power supply and motor speed control device.

Black electric vehicles have wide **application prospects**, and have the advantages of no pollution, low noise and high energy **efficiency**. However, the energy stored per unit weight of the battery is too small, and the continuous **mileage** after charging is not ideal.

composition 组成部分
predetermine 预先确定
be composed of 由……组成
application 应用
prospect 预期
efficiency 效率
mileage 英里

Part Three: Words Study

new energy vehicle 新能源汽车
solar energy 太阳能
fuel cell vehicle 燃料电池车
hybrid 混合动力
hydrogen-power 氢动力
bio fuel 生物燃料
electrical energy 电能
diesel fuel 柴油
combustion 燃烧；氧化
HEV (Hybrid Electric Vehicle) 混合动力汽车
BEV (Blade Electric Vehicle) 纯电动汽车
FCEV (Fuel Cell Electric Vehicle) 燃料电池电动汽车
PHEV (Plug-in Hybrid Electric Vehicle) 插电式混合动力汽车
EV (Electric Vehicle) 电动汽车

Part Four: Knowledge Extension

1. HEV (Hybrid Electric Vehicle): It is a type of hybrid vehicle that combines a conventional internal combustion engine system with an electric propulsion.

Toyota Highlander Hybrid

Fig. 11-8

The Saturn Vue Green Line

Fig. 11-9

2. BEV (Blade Electric Vehicles): This is a type of electric vehicle (EV) that exclusively uses chemical energy stored in rechargeable battery packs. There is no secondary source of propulsion.

BYD E5　　　　　　　　　　　　　　　Aeolus E70

Fig. 11-10　　　　　　　　　　　　　　Fig. 11-11

3. FCEV (Fuel Cell Electric Vehicle): It uses a fuel cell to power its onboard electric motor. Fuel cells often generate electricity from oxygen from air.

Honda Clarity Fuel Cell　　　　　　　　Toyota Mirai

Fig. 11-12　　　　　　　　　　　　　　Fig. 11-13

4. PHEV (Plug-in Hybrid Electric Vehicle): It belongs to hybrid electric vehicle. Its battery can be recharged by plugging it into an external source of electric power.

The Chevrolet Volt　　　　　　　　　　BMW530

Fig. 11-14　　　　　　　　　　　　　　Fig. 11-15

Part Five: Practice

Ⅰ. Translate the following expressions into English.

生物燃料＿＿＿＿＿＿＿＿　　　　　　　电能＿＿＿＿＿＿＿＿＿＿

太阳能_____   混合动力_____
汽油_____   柴油_____
氢动力_____   燃油电池车_____

Ⅱ. Words puzzle.

aut__mo__ile   el__ct__ic__l   c__mpo__it__on
tr__ns__iss__on   ap__lic__tion   h__br__d
pre__et__rmine   in__er__al   p__os__ect

Ⅲ. Write the full name of the abbreviation and translate them into Chinese.

HEV _____
BEV _____
FCEV _____
PHEV _____
EV _____

Ⅳ. Answer the following questions.

1. What are the fuels of new energy vehicles?
_____
2. What are the compositions of electric vehicles?
_____
3. What are the advantages of blade electric vehicles?
_____

Module Two
Business English

商务英语

Module Two Business English 商务英语

Lesson 1

Customer Development

Learning Objectives

Master the basic knowledge and skills	
➢ Language learning objective	Grasp the new words and useful expressions.
➢ Skill learning objective	Be able to introduce automobiles in different ways.
Develop core competences of English	
➢ Know the culture and emotions conveyed by different texts on "Customer Development" topic. ➢ Know the differences between Chinese and Western thinking in English expression. ➢ Develop the pragmatic competence in customer development scene.	

Part One: Warming-up

Make your choice:

1. As a salesman, what do you think about developing/prospecting new customers?
   (　　) Waiting in **4S store**.
   (　　) **Introduced** by regular customers.
   (　　) Holding events to attract interested customers.

   What else?

2. As a salesman, what will you do to turn your customers' good will into sales?
   (　　) Make phone calls to them.
   (　　) Make **appointments** with them.
   (　　) Never **give up** if they **refuse** you.
   (　　) Visit them.

   What else?

4S store 4S 店
introduce 介绍

turn...into...
把……变成……
will 意向
appointment 约会
sale 购买
give up 放弃
refuse 拒绝

3. As a salesman, what will you do when you make an appointment with your customer?

(　) Make a phone call to make sure the time and the place.

(　) Wait for him at the **given place**.

(　) Have a pleasant talk with him.

(　) Thank him at last.

What else?

_____

given place 指定地点

detailed 详细的

As a salesman, you should：

1. Be prepared before visiting customers.
2. Make a return visit to track the customers.
3. Make a **detailed** record about the reception telephones.

Part Two：New Words and Useful Expressions

Ⅰ. New words.

auto	***n.*** 汽车
sale	***n. & v.*** 销售
convenient	***adj.*** 方便的
explanation	***n.*** 讲解
detail	***n.*** 细节
inform	***v.*** 告知
dial	***v.*** 拨打电话
order	***v.*** 订购
disturb	***v.*** 打扰
definitely	***adv.*** 明确地
suggestion	***n.*** 建议
appointment	***n.*** 预约
choice	***n.*** 选择
fit	***v.*** 供给，适应

Module Two Business English 商务英语

Ⅱ. Useful expressions.

1. Don't I know you?
2. I've heard a great deal about you.
3. I can't thank you enough.
4. You have made a good choice.
5. Thank you for your spending so much time answering my questions.
6. Don't forget I'll invite you out to dinner tonight.
7. Shall we say seven o'clock?
8. I'm sorry to take you so long time.
9. Shall we fix a time for a talk?
10. A friend of mine recommended you.

1. 我好像认识您。
2. 久仰大名。
3. 真不知道该如何感谢您。
4. 您的眼力不错。
5. 谢谢您花那么多时间回答我的问题。
6. 别忘了今晚我邀请你吃饭。
7. 那说好七点钟,行吗?
8. 很抱歉占用你这么长时间。
9. 我们能约个时间谈谈吗?
10. 我的一个朋友推荐我来找你。

Part Three: Situations

Situation A

May I speak to …?

> Ms. Liu is making a phone call. She wants to inform Mr. Brown of taking his car, but she dials Mrs. Smith's number.

(L—Ms. Liu, J—Jane, S—Smith)

L: Hello, this is Liu Yan from JiHeng Auto Sales Company. May I speak to Mr. Brown? The car he ordered is ready now.

J: I'm afraid that you dialed a wrong number. We haven't ordered a car.

L: Really?

J: Yeah, my husband didn't tell me that.

L: Just a minute. Is it the phone number of Mr. Brown?

J: No, it's Smith's. I'm Jane Smith.

L: I'm sorry for disturbing you, Mrs. Smith.

J: It doesn't matter.

L: Mrs. Smith, we currently have a new energy electric car for sale in our store, which is very **cost-effective**. Don't you **take an interest in** buying a new car?

J: Yes, but I have to **talk** it **over** with my husband.

cost-effective 划算
take an interest in... 对……有兴趣
talk over 详尽地商议

L: Oh, I see. When is it all right to call your husband?

J: He usually gets home at six.

L: I see, thank you. I'll ring you back later, and I wish I won't disturb your dinner.

J: Well, we often have dinner around half past six.

L: Thank you. I'll call you again later.

(After six o'clock, Ms. Liu calls the Smiths' again)

L: Hello, Mr. Smith, please? I called your wife right this afternoon, and she told me to phone you at this time of the day. So, do you plan to buy a new energy electric car?

S: Well, can you introduce it?

L: Our store has an electric car which is very cost-effective. When will you be free to come to our 4S store? I will introduce it to you **in detail**.

S: I will be free next weekend.

L: I see. I'll **keep in touch with** you. See you next week.

in detail 详细地

keep in touch with 保持联系

 Notes

1. JiHeng Auto Sales Company: 吉亨汽车销售公司。
2. Hello, Mr. Smith, Please? 你好,你是史密斯先生吧?

 Make your choice according to situation A.

	Questions	Answers
(　)	1. Does Ms. Liu dial a wrong number?	A. Mrs. Smith.
(　)	2. Who receives the phone call?	B. No, she doesn't.
(　)	3. Did Mr. and Mrs. Smith order a car?	C. Yes, she does.
(　)	4. Does Ms. Liu give up her call?	D. After six o'clock.
(　)	5. When does Ms. Liu phone Mr. Smith?	E. No, they didn't.

Situation B

Are you free tomorrow morning or afternoon?

Liu Yan is making an appointment with Mr. Hunter by phone.

(L—Ms. Liu, H—Mr. Hunter)

L: Hello, could I speak to Mr. Hunter?

H: This is Hunter speaking.

L: Mr. Hunter, this is Liu Yan from JiHeng Auto Sales Company. Yesterday you came to our company for **information**. You showed great interest in our cars, but left at once.

H: Yes, I had a call then and I had to leave. **Go ahead**.

L: So, Mr. Hunter, which model do you prefer, a fuel car or an electric car?

H: I want to buy a fuel car. I am interested in Aeolus AX7.

L: You have **made** a good **choice**. We can definitely fit your needs, and can I make a suggestion?

H: Sure. What is it?

L: If it is convenient for you tomorrow, you can come to our store. I'll give you a detailed explanation. In this way, you can have a better idea of the car. Do you **agree with** me?

H: Yes, how much time will it take?

L: No more than 60 minutes. Will you be free on tomorrow morning or afternoon?

H: Afternoon is better for me.

L: Would 14∶30 be all right?

H: It's OK.

L: Good. I will wait for you in the store tomorrow afternoon. See you!

H: See you!

information 资料

go ahead 继续

make a choice 选择

agree with 同意

Notes

1. Aeolus Ax7 风神 Ax7
2. How much time will it take? 要花多少时间?

Make your choice according to situation B.

	Questions	Answers
(　)	1. Who is Ms. Liu speaking to?	A. He is interested in a fuel car.
(　)	2. Why does Ms. Liu call Mr. Hunter?	B. At 14∶30 tomorrow afternoon.
(　)	3. Which model does Mr. Hunter prefer?	C. Mr. Hunter.
(　)	4. Why does Ms. Liu invite Mr. Hunter to the store?	D. Because Mr. Hunter came to the 4S store yesterday.
(　)	5. When will Mr. Hunter be free?	E. For a detailed explanation.

Part Four: Practice

Ⅰ. Complete these sentences with the words in the box.

> services, inform, needs, idea, disturbing, appointment, ordered, information, dial, convenient

1. She will _____ Mr. Brown to take his car.
2. She feels sorry for _____ you.
3. She is making an _____ with Mr. Hunter.
4. We can fit your _____.
5. The car which he _____ yesterday is right here.
6. If it is _____ for you, I will visit you.
7. The telephone number you _____ is wrong.
8. Yesterday you came to our store for _____.
9. I'd like to explain our _____ to you.
10. You can have a better _____ of the car.

Ⅱ. Match the following Chinese with English expressions.

( )	1. 继续	A. make an appointment
( )	2. 建议	B. go ahead
( )	3. 定一个约会	C. make a suggestion
( )	4. 保持联系	D. make a phone call
( )	5. 打电话	E. keep in touch with

Ⅲ. Put the following sentences into English.

1. 你今天有空还是明天有空?（Will you be free...）
2. 我们能完全满足您的需求。（We can definitely...）
3. 我会向您详细介绍。（I will...）
4. 难道您对购买新车不感兴趣吗?（Don't you take...）
5. 我希望将不会打扰你们吃饭。（I wish...）
6. 我会和你保持联系的。（I will...）

Ⅳ. Complete the following tasks.

1. Play the parts in the dialogues.
2. Make a dialogue according to the next situation: Supposing a customer shows

great interest in your cars, he doesn't tell you if he wants to buy, and then he leaves the store. Now you phone him.

Ⅴ. Self-check.

I learned:
( ) appointment   ( ) recommend   ( ) inform   ( ) development
( ) dial   ( ) suggestion   ( ) choice   ( ) refuse
( ) detail   ( ) ring   ( ) auto   ( ) model

I can:
( ) make phone calls.
( ) introduce myself.
( ) make appointments.

Lesson 2

Customer Reception

 Learning Objectives

Master the basic knowledge and skills	
➤ Language learning objective	Grasp the new words and useful expressions.
➤ Skill learning objective	Be able to greet customers and meet customers' special needs.
Develop core competences of English	
➤ Know the culture and emotions conveyed by different texts on "Customer Reception" topic. ➤ Know the differences between Chinese and Western thinking in English expression. ➤ Develop the pragmatic competence in information collection scene.	

customer 客户
meet 迎合，满足

Part One: Warming-up

Make your choice:

1. As a customer, when you walk into a 4S store, you hope:
   (　　) The **salesman** will greet you.
   (　　) You will be served politely.
   (　　) The salesman won't disturb your visit.
   (　　) The salesman will have detailed **instructions** of the car you **are interested in**.

   What else?

salesman 销售员
instruction 说明
be interested in
对……感兴趣
receive 接待

2. As a salesman, what will you do when you receive a customer?
   (　　) Welcome him/her.
   (　　) Greet him/her and his/her friends.
   (　　) Hand a cup of tea or coffee.
   (　　) **Observe** what he/she cares about.

observe 观察

Module Two Business English 商务英语

( ) Look at him/her while you are talking.
( ) **Judge** him/her with his/her **appearance**.

 What else?

judge 判断
appearance 外表

3. As a salesman, do you know what you shouldn't do when you receive a customer?
( ) Smoking
( ) Walking around with a cup of coffee.
( ) Standing against a car.
( ) **Staring at** your client up and down.

 What else?

stare at 盯着

 As a salesman, you should pay attention to:

1. Greet customers proactively, introduce yourself and hand in your business card
2. Keep an appropriate distance from customers and pay attention to customers' needs.
3. Give the information to customers, and talk about the topics that customers are interested in.
4. Say goodbye to customers at the door of 4S store, make an appointment for the next visit, and watch customers leave.
5. Be ready to welcome other customers.

Part Two: New Words and Useful Expressions

Ⅰ. New words.

showroom	***n***. 展厅
receive	***v***. 接待
realistic	***adj***. 现实的
probably	***adv***. 可能地
prefer	***v***. 更喜欢
suit	***v***. 适合
bet	***v***. 打赌
definitely	***adv***. 肯定地,明确地
serve	***v***. 服务,招待

75

Ⅱ. Useful expressions.

1. Welcome to our motor shop.
2. What can I do for you?
3. Please come in.
4. Would you like a cup of tea?
5. Do you sell the red cars?
6. May I know your name?
7. Is this your first time to visit our showroom?
8. Be sure to call me if you need any help.
9. Can I show you around?
10. I'm just looking around.

1. 欢迎光临本店。
2. 能为您效劳吗?
3. 请进!
4. 来杯咖啡吗?
5. 这里有红色的车卖吗?
6. 能认识一下吗?
7. 您是第一次到我们展厅吧?
8. 如有什么需要,请叫我。
9. 我来带您四处看看好吗?
10. 我只是看看而已。

Part Three：Situations

Situation A

I also enjoy self-driving tour

Mr. Gray comes to a 4S store.
Ms. Liu, a saleswoman, receives him.

（L—Ms. Liu, G—Gray）

L：Good morning. Welcome to our 4S store.

G：Morning.

L：I am Liu Yan, the saleswoman of this store. May I know your name?

G：I'm Geoffrey Gray. I like to travel by car on weekends and want to buy a **fuel-efficient** car. Can you recommend a car that suits me?

L：My pleasure. Aeolus E70 is the **best-selling** model in our store. This car is a new energy electric car. It saves energy and protects environment, whose battery life is 500km, with 10-year **warranty** and unlimited **mileage**. This car is very suitable for you to travel on the weekend.

G：Sounds great. Are there other electric cars in your store?

L：There is also a car called Aeolus Yixuan EV. The appearance of this car is very fashionable and the interior is comfortable. This car is very suitable for a fashionable person like you. If you are interested, you can experience it in the car. I bet you'll definitely like it.

G：Really? I will take a closer look.

fuel-efficient 省油的

best-selling 畅销

be suitable for 适合……
warranty 担保,授权
mileage 英里数

Module Two Business English 商务英语

 Notes

1. 4S store：4S 店。4S 指 sale（整车销售）、sparepart（零件配供应）、service（售后服务）、survey（信息反馈）。
2. SUV：全称是 Sport Utility Vehicle，即"运动型多功能车"。

 Make your choice according to situation A.

	Questions	Answers
( )	1. What does Liu Yan do?	A. Good morning. Welcome to our motor shop.
( )	2. How does Liu Yan greet Mr. Gray?	B. New energy electric car.
( )	3. Why does Mr. Gray want to buy a fuel-efficient car?	C. Aeolus ETO.
( )	4. What car does Mr. Gray prefer?	D. He likes to travel by car on weekends.
( )	5. Which is the best-selling Model in the 4S store?	E. She is a saleswoman of a 4S store.

Situation B

Where do you work?

Mr. Black, a worker, comes to a 4S store and Ms. Liu receives him.

（L—Ms. Liu，B—Mr. Black）

L：Good afternoon, sir. Welcome to our 4S store.

B：Good afternoon.

L：I'm Liu Yan, the saleswoman. I hope you'll enjoy my service. May I know your name?

B：My name is Jim Black.

L：Nice to meet you, Mr. Black. You must be a teacher, am I right?

B：No, I'm not. In fact, I'm a worker and I work in an iron and steel company.

L：Have you ever been to our store?

B：No, but I've been to several stores already.

L：What type of car do you **have in mind**?

have in mind 考虑

search for 查找

B: I prefer a SUV. And the trunk capacity of the car should be large.

L: Well, it's lucky for you to come to our store. Look, doesn't that SUV suit for you?

B: This car, I know. I have **searched for** information about the car on the Internet.

L: I believe you should have a certain understanding of this car, but 80% of the car's performance requires a test drive to experience. If you have time, I can arrange a test drive for you.

B: That couldn't be better.

L: Excuse me, have you brought your driver's license?

B: Of course.

L: Okay, please come here for the test drive procedures.

 Notes

1. iron and steel company：钢铁公司。
2. It's lucky for you to come to our store. 您来这儿很幸运。

 Make your choice according to situation B.

	Questions	Answers
( )	1. Where does Mr. Black work?	A. A worker.
( )	2. What type of car does Mr. Black have in mind?	B. No.
( )	3. What does Mr. Black do?	C. She asks Mr. Black whether he is a teacher.
( )	4. Does Ms. Liu want to visit Mr. Black?	D. SUV.
( )	5. How does Ms. Liu begin his talk?	E. In an iron and steel company.

Part Four: Practice

Ⅰ. Complete these sentences with the words in the box.

> saleswoman, iron, steel, bet, company, cloudy, service, type, like, worker, store, trip, fishing

1. I've been at the _____ since this afternoon.
2. Ms. Liu is a _____ of a 4S store.

3. It is _____ now and it may rain tomorrow.
4. Mr. Gray enjoys _____ and a weekend _____.
5. What _____ of car does Mr. Gray like?
6. I _____ you will like the car.
7. I will serve you and you will enjoy my _____.
8. I work in an _____ and _____ company.
9. Mr. Black looks _____ a teacher and he doesn't look like a _____.
10. Welcome to our 4S _____.

Ⅱ. Match the following Chinese with English expressions.

( )	1. 销售员	A. customer reception
( )	2. 顾客接待	B. SUV
( )	3. 运动型多用途车	C. salesman
( )	4. 试驾	D. a test drive
( )	5. 4S 店	E. 4S Store

Ⅲ. Put the following sentences into English.

1. 欢迎光临本店。(Welcome to...)
2. 明天很可能会出太阳。(Tomorrow will be...)
3. 您想买什么车？(What type of car...?)
4. 您想要这辆运动型多功能车吗？(Do you... in mind)
5. 接待您这样的顾客真是我的幸运。(It's lucky for me to...)
6. 我很喜欢跑步。(I enjoy doing...)

Ⅳ. Complete the following tasks.

1. Play the parts in the dialogues.
2. Make dialogues according to the next situations：Supposing a business man, a doctor or a salesman comes to your 4S store, you receive them.

Ⅴ. Self-check.

I learned：
( ) salesman   ( ) show around   ( ) serve   ( ) showroom
( ) 4S store   ( ) receive   ( ) workshop   ( ) iron
( ) steel   ( ) probably   ( ) arrange   ( ) suit

I can：
( ) greet customers and begin talks.
( ) meet customers' special needs.
( ) receive some customers.

Lesson 3

Information Collection

Learning Objectives

Master the basic knowledge and skills	
➢ Language learning objective	Grasp the new words and useful expressions.
➢ Skill learning objective	Be able to get more information from customers.
Develop core competences of English	
➢ Know the culture and emotions conveyed by different texts on "Information Collection" topic. ➢ Know the differences between Chinese and Western thinking in English expression. ➢ Develop the pragmatic competence in information collection scene.	

Part One: Warming-up

collect 收集
information 信息

provide 提供

prepare 准备

write down 记下

___ Make your choice:

1. Why is it important for a salesman to **collect information**?
   (　) For knowing about customers' needs.
   (　) For developing customers.
   (　) For **providing** better service for customers.
   (　) For selling more cars.

2. As a salesman, what will you **prepare** before you collect information?
   (　) General questions.
   (　) Specific questions.
   (　) A note book to **write down** the information.

Module Two Business English 商务英语

(　) The thanks in the end.

What else?

3. Which **main** information will you collect?
(　) Names.
(　) Age.
(　) **Hobbies**.
(　) Telephone numbers.
(　) **Occupations**.

What else?

main 主要的

hobby 爱好

occupation 职业

 When you collect information, you should:

1. Talk in good manners.
2. Never mention the **privacy**.

privacy 隐私

Part Two: New Words and Useful Expressions

I. New words.

purchase	*n.* 购买
sedan	*n.* 小轿车
control	*v.* 控制
condition	*n.* 状况
lawyer	*n.* 律师
run	*v.* 运行
main	*adj.* 主要的
worn	*adj.* 破旧
make	*n.* 牌子
hybrid	*n.* 混合

81

Ⅱ. Useful expressions.

1. Do you mind a few questions of mine?
2. Do you go to work by car?
3. What make is your car?
4. How many years have you had your car?
5. Who uses the car, you or your wife?
6. When will you buy another car?
7. How is your car running?
8. Do you like a sedan or an SUV?
9. What do you do in your spare time?
10. What are the main problems with your car?

1. 我问您几个问题您不介意吧？
2. 您是开车上班吗？
3. 您的车是什么牌子？
4. 您的车开了多少年了？
5. 您家车主要谁在用，是您还是您夫人？
6. 您何时再买车？
7. 您的车跑得怎么样？
8. 您喜欢轿车还是运动型多功能车？
9. 您空闲的时候都干什么？
10. 您的车主要有什么问题？

Part Three：Situations

Situation A

Do you like a new energy car?

> Mr. Dodd enters a 4S store. Liu Yan receives him and asks him some questions.

(L—Ms. Liu，D—Mr. Dodd)

L：What can I do for you, sir?
D：I'd like to have a look first.
L：May I know when you will use a car?
D：In the new year. I think it is a new beginning.
L：Good idea! So who is going to use the car?
D：My wife.
L：I guess your wife is a woman who **is succesful in** her career, right?
D：She is a salesman. As a salesman, you know, she has a long way to go every day.
L：Does she like a **new energy** car?
D：Of course.
L：Well, electric cars have low noise and high energy efficiency. It's perfect for

---

be succesful in
在…方面成功

new energy car
新能源汽车

your wife. What color does she like?

D: White.

L: Does she like a sedan or an SUV?

D: A sedan.

L: What about hybrid cars?

D: No, she prefers blade electric cars.

L: That's right. Now is a very good time to buy blade electric cars. The technology is mature, the charging piles are popular, and the purchase tax is free. Look at that car. We just have one that meets your needs.

Notes

1. What about hybird cars? 喜欢混合动力车吗？what about 表示征求意见。
2. Electric cars have low noise and high energy efficiency. 电动车具有低噪声，高能效。

 Make your choice according to situation A.

	Questions	Answers
(　)	1. Does Mr. Dodd want to buy a car?	A. In the new year.
(　)	2. When does Mr. Dodd use his car?	B. No, he doesn't.
(　)	3. Who will use his car?	C. Yes, she does.
(　)	4. Does Mr. Dodd need a sedan or an SUV?	D. Mr. Dodd's wife.
(　)	5. Does Mrs. Dodd like hybrid cars?	E. A sedan.

Situation B

Your car is in poor condition.

> Liu Yan is talking with Mr. Collins for more information.

(L—Ms. Liu, C Mr. Collins)

L: Hello, I'm Liu Yan. May I know your name?

C: Hi, I am Jim Collins.

L: Do you mind a few questions of mine?

C: Not at all. Go ahead, please.

L: How many people are there in your family?

C: Four. I have two children.

L: Oh, I think you must be a good father, and spend much time with your children.

C: No, I'm a lawyer and I am very busy. But on weekends, I drive my family to the countryside.

L: How is your car running?

C: Not very well. It has run for 8 years.

L: What are the main problems with your car?

C: It's **worn out** and needs a lot of repairs. My car doesn't have a navigation system, and it is very inconvenient to go out for a self-driving tour.

L: At present, many cars are equipped with "Intelligent Vehicle System", which brings a lot of convenience and entertainment for driving. What about the engine?

C: The **driving power** is not strong and it doesn't start quickly enough.

L: Oh, your car is now **in poor condition**. Are you considering changing a new car now?

C: Of course. The sooner, the better.

worn out 磨损，很旧
driving power 驱动力
in poor condition 车况很差

Make your choice according to situation B.

	Questions	Answers
( )	1. How many children does Mr. Collins have?	A. It's not strong and doesn't start quickly.
( )	2. What does Mr. Collins do?	B. Two.
( )	3. How is Mr. Collins' car?	C. Yes, he does.
( )	4. How is the engine of Mr. Collins' car?	D. A lawyer.
( )	5. Does Mr. Collins like self-driving?	E. It's worn out.

Part Four: Practice

Ⅰ. Complete these sentences with the words in the box.

> repairs, poor, sedan, kind, start, mind, meet, blade, electric, business, running

1. My wife needs a _____.
2. She likes _____ cars.
3. My car is now in _____ condition.
4. We just have cars that _____ her needs.

5. My car is worn out and needs a lot of _____.
6. Do you _____ a few questions of mine?
7. The car has run for some years and doesn't _____ quickly enough.
8. How is your car _____?
9. What _____ of car do you like?
10. Here is my _____ card.

Ⅱ. Match the following Chinese with English expressions.

( )	1. 名片	A. main problems
( )	2. 快速起动	B. blade electric cars
( )	3. 主要问题	C. air-conditioner
( )	4. 纯电动车	D. business card
( )	5. 空调	E. start quickly

Ⅲ. Put the following sentences into English.

1. 您是需要轿车还是运动型多功能车。（Do you need...）
2. 他喜欢带混合动力的轿车吗？（Does he like...）
3. 您的车况已经很差了。（Your car is...）
4. 您介意我提几个问题吗？（Do you mind...）
5. 您喜欢什么牌子的车？（What make....）
6. 您的车况如何？（How is.... running）

Ⅳ. Complete the following tasks.

1. Play the parts in the dialogues.
2. Make a dialogue according to the next situation：Supposing a customer comes to the 4S store, you want to get some information from him/her, and then you ask him/her some questions.

Ⅴ. Self-check.

I learned：
( ) sedan   ( ) condition   ( ) SUV   ( ) automatic
( ) hybrid cars ( ) make   ( ) worn   ( ) collection

I can：
( ) know about customers' needs.
( ) provide better services for customers.

Lesson 4

Automobile Introduction

Learning Objectives:

Master the basic knowledge and skills	
➢ Language learning objective	Grasp the new words and useful expressions.
➢ Skill learning objectives	1. Be able to introduce automobiles in different ways. 2. Use FAB principle to introduce an automobile.
Develop core competences of English	

➢ Know the culture and emotions conveyed by different texts on "Automobile Introduction" topic.
➢ Know the differences between Chinese and Western thinking in English expression.
➢ Develop the pragmatic competence in automobile introduction scene.

Part One: Warming-up

Make your choice

1. As a salesman, how will you make an automobile **introduction**?
   (　) I can introduce the equipment and advantages of automobiles.
   (　) I can explain different functions **in detail**.
   (　) I can ask the customers to operate the car by themselves.
   (　) I can provide some related information to customers.

   What else? _____

2. As a customer, what would you like to know when you want to buy a new car?
   (　) The **dimensions** of the car.
   (　) **Performance**.
   (　) **Safety equipment**.

introduction 介绍

dimension 尺寸
performance 性能
safety equipment 安全配置

( ) **Comfort** and **convenience**.

What else?

comfort 舒适
convenience 方便

3. As a salesman, how will you answer customers' questions?
( ) By introducing it with patience.
( ) By making a brief introduction.
( ) By giving an example
( ) By comparing with another model.

What else?

 You should pay attention to:

FAB principle in motor explanation:

 F→ **Feature**
 A→ **Advantage**
 B→ **Benefit**

 How to explain ABS in FAB way?

feature 配置
advantage 优势
benefit 利益

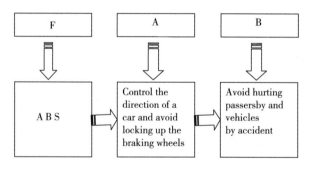

Part Two: New Words and Useful Expressions

Ⅰ. New words.

captivate	*v.* 使迷住
spacious	*adj.* 宽广的
interaction	*n.* 相互影响

87

elaborate on	*v.* 详细描述
terminal	*n.* 终端机
automatically	*adv.* 自动地
multiple	*adj.* 多样的
navigation	*n.* 航行
hardware	*n.* 硬件
concise	*adj.* 简明的
overvalue	*n.* 超值
device	*n.* 装置
park	*v.* 停车
control	*v.* 控制
maximum	*adj.* 最大的

Ⅱ. Useful expressions.

1. How is the car's fuel efficiency?
2. This car only uses unleaded gasoline.
3. Is there a rear window defroster?
4. Is rust-proofing a standard feature?
5. How many cylinders does this engine have?
6. What standard features are included in this model?
7. Is the transmission manual or automatic?
8. How many miles per gallon can this car go?
9. This car is very easy to drive. It has power steering wheel and brake booster.
10. The new model features some new equipments.

1. 这部车燃油效率怎样？
2. 这部车只能用无铅汽油。
3. 有后窗除霜装置吗？
4. 防锈是标准设置吗？
5. 这部发动机有多少个气缸？
6. 这种车型包含了什么标准设置？
7. 变速器是手动的还是自动的？
8. 这部车每加仑油能跑多少公里？
9. 这部车很容易驾驶。它有助力转向和制动助力装置。
10. 这款新车的亮点是安装了一些新设备。

Module Two Business English 商务英语

Part Three: Situations

Situation A

Which car are you interested in?

Mr. Lu is introducing the car to Mr. Ford...

(L—Mr. Lu, F—Mr. Ford)

L: Mr. Ford, which car are you interested in?
F: I am captivated by Aeolus AX7, could you please introduce it to me?
L: Of course. First of all, it is a 5-seat SUV with a length of 4645mm and a wheelbase of 2715mm. Its ride space is very spacious. In addition, the central control screen of this car is a 10.25-inch **touch screen**, which can realize intelligent dual-screen interaction with an **Intelligent Vehicle System**.
F: Excuse me, could you elaborate on the Intelligent Vehicle System? I **am** very **absorbed in** it.
L: Yes, of course. The Intelligent Vehicle System has a terminal with multiple functions such as ETC, 5G **wireless communication**, GPS navigation, travel guide, shopping, entertainment, audio and video, etc. This AX7 is equipped with WindLink3.0 artificial intelligence vehicle system, with high hardware configuration, concise UI experience, and extremely speedy AI voice. It can be controlled by voice, making it safer and more convenient while driving. In the meanwhile, WindLink3.0 can also be automatically interconnected with smart products such as mobile phones, making more entertainment.
F: It sounds great. I can't wait to experience it.
L: Of course, you can get in the car to experience it yourself.

touch screen 触摸屏
Intelligent Vehicle System 智能车机系统

be absorbed in 对…着迷

wireless communication 无线通信

interconnect with 互相联系

 Notes

1. ETC: Electronic Toll Collection 不停车收费系统
2. GPS: Global Positioning System 全球定位系统
3. AI: Artificial Intelligence 人工智能

89

Make your choice according to situation A.

	Questions	Answers
( )	1. Which car is Mr. Ford interested in?	A. 4645mm.
( )	2. What's the length of the SUV?	B. Aeolus AX7.
( )	3. What's the speciality of the Intelligent Vehicle System?	C. ETC, 5G wireless communication, GPS navigation and so on.
( )	4. What is included in the Intelligent Vehicle System?	D. Yes, he is.
( )	5. Is Mr. Ford captivated by the car?	E. It has a terminal with multiple functions.

Situation B

May I ask you some questions?

Mr. Jones is going to buy a car. He is asking Mr. Lu some questions.

(L—Mr. Lu, J—Mr. Jones)

J: Can I ask you some questions, Mr. Lu?

L: Yes, please.

J: What is the **fuel consumption** of the car?

L: It is 7.0L/100km (MT) or 7.2L/100km (AT).

J: What's the **maximum speed**?

L: It's 195km/h (MT) or 180km/h (AT).

J: Is the car rear-wheel drive, front-wheel drive or four-wheel drive?

L: It is rear-wheel drive.

J: Does the engine have four cylinders or six cylinders?

L: It has four cylinders.

J: Is the engine the inline, V-type or **flat arrangement**?

L: It's inline arrangement.

J: What is the cylinder **displacement**?

L: It is 1.6 liters.

J: How about the transmission of the car?

L: It has five **manual gears** and four **automatic gears**.

fuel consumption 油耗
MT mannual transmission 手动档
AT automatic transmission 自动档
maximum speed 最高时速

flat arrangement 水平对置

displacement 排气量

manual gear 手动档
automatic gear 自动档

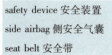

J: What **safety devices** is the car equipped with?
L: It has twin front airbags, **side airbags**, **seat belts**, ABS, EBD, ASR and so on.
J: OK. Thank you very much.
L: You are welcome.

safety device 安全装置
side airbag 侧安全气囊
seat belt 安全带

 Notes

1. twin front airbags：驾驶人及前排乘客安全气囊
2. EBD：Electrical Brake Device，电子制动装置
3. ASR：Anti-Spin Regulation，驱动防滑系统
4. Is the engine the inline, V-type or flat arrangement? 发动机是直列式、V形排列还是水平对置排列？

 Make your choice according to situation B.

	Questions	Answers
( )	1. What is the fuel consumption?	A. Four cylinders
( )	2. How many manual gears does the car have?	B. Inline.
( )	3. What is the displacement?	C. 7.0L/100km (MT) or 7.2L/100km (AT).
( )	4. Is the engine V-type or inline?	D. Five.
( )	5. Does the engine have six cylinders or four cylinders?	E. 1.6 liters.

Part Four: Practice

Ⅰ. Complete these sentences with the words in the box.

> speed, displacement, multiple, consumption, manual, captivated, navigation, automatic, elaborate, device

1. I'm _____ by this car.
2. The car is equipped with_____ functions.
3. Could you_____ on its ABS?
4. Side airbags belong to safety _____.

5. What is the fuel _____ of the car?

6. The maximum _____ of the car is 195km/h（MT）.

7. The cylinder _____ of the car is 1.6litres.

8. The car has five _____ gears and four automatic gears.

9. The car is famous for its _____ driving technique.

10. GPS _____ is necessary for a car.

Ⅱ. Match the following Chinese with English expressions.

( )	1. 车辆的安全性	A. power and operation
( )	2. 动力与操控	B. the safety of the car
( )	3. 四轮驱动	C. a braking wheel
( )	4. 制动轮	D. front airbags
( )	5. 前排安全气囊	E. four-wheel drive

Ⅲ. Put the following sentences into English.

1. 本车的油耗是自动档每百公里7.2升。(The fuel consumption is...)

2. 本车的发动机有四个气缸。(The engine of the car...)

3. 本车的最大速度是手动档每小时195公里。(The maximum speed of...)

4. 本车装有ETC通行、5G无线通信、GPS导航等多功能的车载终端。(...is equipped with)

5. 该车是一款5座SUV，车长4445mm，车轴距2175mm。(...with a length of... and a wheelbase of...)

6. WindLink3.0可以与手机等智能产品产生互联。(be interconnected with...)

Ⅳ. Complete the following tasks.

1. Play the parts in the dialogues.

2. Make a dialogue according to the next situation：Supposing a customer comes to your store, he asks you many questions about a car's performance.

Ⅴ. Self-check.

I learned：

( ) captivate　　( ) spacious　　( ) device　　( ) interaction

( ) terminal　　( ) automatically　　( ) navigation　　( ) hardware

( ) intelligent　　( ) manual　　( ) speed　　( ) maximum

I can：

( ) introduce a car.

( ) answer customers' questions about automobiles.

( ) use FAB principle to introduce a car.

Module Two Business English 商务英语

Lesson 5

Price Discussion

Learning Objectives:

Master the basic knowledge and skills	
➢ Language learning objective	Grasp the new words and useful expressions.
➢ Skill learning objectives	1. Be able to deal with customers' inquire. 2. Persuade customers to accept your price.
Develop core competences of English	
➢ Know the culture and emotions conveyed by different texts on "Price Discussion" topic. ➢ Know the differences between Chinese and Western thinking in English expression. ➢ Develop the pragmatic competence in price discussion scene.	

Part One: Warming-up

Make your choice:

1. As a salesman, how will you deal with it when a customer asks about the price?
   (　) Give him/her a price list.
   (　) Refuse to tell him/her the price unless he ensures to buy it.
   (　) Ask if he/she really wants it.
   (　) Ignore his/her demands.

   What else? _____

2. As a salesman, how will you persuade your customer to accept your price?
   (　) Introduce the qualities of the car.
   (　) Tell him/her the benefits of buying the car.
   (　) Compare it with other prices.

compare with 比较

(   ) Analyze the advantages of the car.

3. If a customer really wants your car, how will you give him a **satisfactory** price?
(   ) Give him/her a discount according to the **policy**.
(   ) **Promise** him/her some **accessories** freely.
(   ) Promise him/her good service after selling.
(   ) Agree on the price he/she wants.

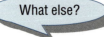

 When you persuade your customer to buy a car:

1. You should **insist on** your stand.
2. You should be **flexible** to give some discount.
3. You should never be afraid of being refused.
4. You can never compel customers to make a decision.

---

satisfactory 满意的
policy 政策
promise 承诺
accessories 附件

insist on 坚持
flexible 灵活的

Part Two: New Words and Useful Expressions

Ⅰ. New words.

interrupt	*v.* 打扰
economy	*n.* 经济
discuss	*v.* 讨论
sales drive	*n.* 促销
postpone	*v.* 推迟
discount	*n.* 折扣
promise	*n&v.* 承诺
budget	*n.* 预算
frankly	*adv.* 坦率地
accept	*v.* 接受
expect	*v.* 期待
persuade	*v.* 说服
bargain	*n.* 交易

Module Two Business English 商务英语

Ⅱ. Useful expressions.

1. You get what you pay for.	1. 一分钱一分货。
2. The prices are fixed, and we have no second price.	2. 我们按定价卖，我们不还价。
3. The car is on sale.	3. 该车特价销售。
4. Let's meet half way.	4. 我们可以各让一半。
5. I can give you a two percent discount.	5. 我可以打百分之二的折扣。
6. A three percent discount is not a small amount.	6. 百分之三的折扣已经不少了。
7. We don't allow a discount.	7. 我们不打折。
8. It's far below our cost price.	8. 这远低于我们的成本价。
9. The cost of production has been skyrocketing.	9. 生产成本在飞涨。
10. This is the lowest price of ours and we are unable to accept a second price.	10. 这是我们的最低报价了，任何还价都无法接受了。

Part Three: Situations

Situation A

What is the price, please?

Mr. Max comes to the 4S store. Lu Zhi is showing a car to him, but Mr. Max interrupts him several times.

(L—Mr. Lu, M—Mr. Max)

L: OK, let's start from the engine.
M: Excuse me, could you tell me the price of the car, please?
L: (Ignoring Mr. Max) The cylinder displacement is 1.6 liters.
M: Can you tell me the price, please?
L: Just a minute, I'll soon **tend to** the price. Now we come to its economy.

tend to 转到

real bargain 合算交易
take it easy 别急

M: What's the price, please?

L: I'll soon move to it, but that is not the most important thing. I just want you to know more about the car, and then you'll certainly find it a **real bargain**. So please **take it easy** and listen to me first, OK?

M: All right.

L: The last point, the maximum speed is 195km/h (MT) and 180km/h (AT). OK, I know you are getting to like the car, and I believe you'll be excited when you find it is a real bargain.

M: Really?

L: All right, the price of the car is ￥132,000.

Notes

1. Ignoring Mr. Max. 不理会马克斯先生。
2. Now we come to its economy. 现在让我们来讲讲该车的经济性。

Make your choice according to situation A.

	Questions	Answers
( )	1. Does Mr. Max interrupt Mr. Lu several times?	A. Yes, he is.
( )	2. How many times does Mr. Max interrupt Mr. Lu?	B. Yes, he can.
( )	3. Can Mr. Lu go on with his introduction?	C. ￥132,000
( )	4. What's the price of the car?	D. Three times.
( )	5. Is Mr. Lu patient?	E. Yes, he does.

Situation B

Can't the price be lower?

Mr. Max is discussing the price with Mr. Lu.

(L—Mr. Lu, M—Mr. Max)

L: Have you decided to buy that model?

M: Yes.

L: Right, Mr. Max. Please come to my office?

M: OK. Do you have a sales drive or a discount for this model?

L: I'm sorry to tell you we have no discount and the sales drive ended yesterday.

M: Can't you postpone it for one day?

L: No. As a famous company, you know, we must **keep** our **promise**. I'm sorry.

M: That's all right.

L: So, what is your budget?

M: Then what's your price?

L: It's ¥132,000.

M: But my budget is ¥130,000.

L: Frankly, we can't accept your price. If we sell it at your price, I'm afraid you won't have some **spare parts**. How about ¥131,500?

M: It's still more than I expected. Can't it be lower?

L: OK, ¥131,000. I can't beat that.

M: All right. It's a deal.

L: Thanks. Do you pay by **credit card** or **in cash**?

M: By credit card.

L: Thanks.

keep promise 信守承诺

spare part 配置

credit card 信用卡
in cash 用现金

 Notes

1. I can't beat that. 我只能出这个价了。
2. It's a deal. 成交。

 Make your choice according to situation B.

	Questions	Answers
( )	1. Has Mr. Max decided to buy a car?	A. No, there is not.
( )	2. Is there any sales drive or discount?	B. ¥131,000.
( )	3. What's Mr. Max's budget?	C. Yes, he has.
( )	4. What's the final deal?	D. ¥130,000.
( )	5. How does Mr. Max pay for the car?	E. By credit card.

Part Four: Practice

Ⅰ. Complete these sentences with the words and phrases in the box.

> interrupting, accept, bargain, sales drive, price, credit card, discuss, budget, promise, parts

1. You'll be excited when you find the price a real _____.
2. Salesmen always _____ the price with customers before deals.
3. I'm very sorry for _____ your introduction.

4. Could you tell me the _____ of the car?

5. We must keep our _____ when we deal with customers.

6. You can buy some _____ in this store.

7. There is a _____ in the store this month.

8. When someone plans to buy a car, he'll have a _____.

9. I can't _____ your price, because it's too low.

10. I'd like to pay for my car by _____.

Ⅱ. Match the following Chinese with English expressions.

( )	1. 讨论价格	A. a fair bargain
( )	2. 很划算	B. discuss the price
( )	3. 备件	C. take it easy
( )	4. 别着急	D. keep promise
( )	5. 遵守承诺	E. spare parts

Ⅲ. Put the following sentences into English.

1. 让我们从发动机开始吧。(Let's...)
2. 您一定会发现它真的很划算。(You'll certainly...)
3. 恐怕你得不到一些配置。(I'm afraid...)
4. 这辆车特价销售。(...on sale)
5. 请别着急。(Please...)
6. 一分钱一分货。(You get...)

Ⅳ. Complete the following tasks.

1. Play the parts in the dialogues.
2. Make a dialogue according to the next situation: Supposing you are discussing the price of a car with a customer.

Ⅴ. Self-check.

I learned：

( ) discuss   ( ) bargain   ( ) interrupt   ( ) budget

( ) economy   ( ) sales   ( ) drive   ( ) discount

( ) promise   ( ) price list   ( ) flexible   ( ) persuade

I can：

( ) tell customers the price smartly.

( ) discuss the price with customers.

( ) persuade customers to accept my price.

Module Two Business English 商务英语

Lesson 6

Delivery of Vehicles

Learning Objectives:

Master the basic knowledge and skills	
➢ Language learning objective	Grasp the new words and useful expressions.
➢ Skill learning objectives	1. Be able to meet the customers' delivery requirements. 2. Make a delivery to customers.
Develop core competences of English	

➢ Know the culture and emotions conveyed by different texts on "Delivery of Vehicles" topic.
➢ Know the differences between Chinese and Western in building a long-term relationship with customers.
➢ Develop the pragmatic competence in delivery of vehicles.

Part One: Warming-up

Make your choice:

1. As a customer, when you walk into a 4S store to get your new car, you hope
   (   ) The salesman will greet you with congratulations.
   (   ) The salesman will introduce the details of delivery process.
   (   ) The salesman will answer your questions about the delivery issues.
   (   ) The salesman will accompany you to inspect your new car.

   What else?
   _____

2. As a salesman, what will you do when you make a delivery to your customer?
   (   ) Prepare the files before the delivery.
   (   ) Make a delivery ceremony for celebration.

( ) Help your customer to complete the forms.

( ) Explain some free projects of vehicle maintenance.

( ) Inspect the new vehicle with your customer.

3. As a salesman, do you know what you shouldn't do when you make a delivery to your customer?

( ) Let your customer check the vehicle alone.

( ) Explain the delivery process roughly.

( ) Refuse to help your customer to complete the files.

( ) Don't phone your customer after delivering.

As a salesman, you should pay attention to:

1. Wait for your customers in the store in advance and greet them proactively.
2. Show your congratulations to your customers and show them the identifications of the vehicle.
3. Accompany your customers to check their new vehicles and make sure there is no damage on it.
4. Make a brief introduction of the delivery process and show them how to fill in the files.
5. Introduce the maintenance process.
6. Make a phone call after car delivery to keep in touch with your customer.

Part Two: New Words and Useful Expressions

Ⅰ. New words.

available	*adj.* 有空的
prepare	*v.* 准备
contract	*n.* 合约

balance	*n.*	余额
inspect	*v.*	检查
defect	*n.*	缺陷
trim	*n.*	汽车装饰
acceptance	*n.*	验收
checklist	*n.*	清单
confirm	*v.*	确认
Bluetooth	*n.*	蓝牙
damage	*n.*	损伤

Ⅱ. Useful expressions.

1. May I ask when you will come to go through the pick-up procedure?
2. Do you need us to provide pick-up service?
3. New cars need running-in.
4. It may take three hours to make the car delivery.
5. New cars need maintaining.
6. Here is your car keys.
7. Mr. Wang, congratulations on your car delivery!
8. Here is the warranty certificate, user's manual and product certification.
9. Please show your car purchase contract.
10. Please thoroughly inspect the vehicle to check it is all correct and without damage before signing the vehicle acceptance note.

1. 请问您什么时候来办理提车手续？
2. 您需要接送服务吗？
3. 新车需要磨合。
4. 提车过程可能花费3个小时。
5. 新车要注意保养。
6. 这是您的车钥匙。
7. 王先生，恭喜您喜提爱车！
8. 这是新车的保修单，用户手册以及产品合格证。
9. 请出示您的购车合同。
10. 请您在签署车辆验收单之前对车辆进行彻底检查，以检查其是否正确且无损坏。

Part Three: Situations

Situation A

When are you available to take delivery of your car?

> Mr. Lu is making a phone call to make sure the car delivery time.

(L—Mr. Lu, W—Mr. Wang)

L: Hello, This is Lu Zhi, May I speak to Mr. Wang?

W: Yes, who is speaking?

L: Good morning, Mr. Wang. I'm the salesman of Audi 4S store. The new car you bought last week has been delivered. Would you tell me when you are available to take delivery of your car?

W: I will **be free** on Sunday.

L: OK. We need to do PDI inspection before delivery. In addition, we'll make a thorough cleaning for the new car. So, how about 11:00 on Sunday morning?

W: It's OK.

L: Do you need us to provide **pick-up service**?

W: No, thanks. I can go there by taxi. What do I need to prepare for the delivery?

L: Please take your own ID card, the contract and the **balance payment** of the car **in advance**.

W: How much time should I **set aside** for the delivery process?

L: The delivery process mainly includes vehicle inspection and operation, final payment, file filling and delivery ceremony. It will take at least 3 hours. Please give yourself as much time as necessary.

W: OK. See you at 11:00 on Sunday morning.

L: **I'm looking forward to** seeing you! Goodbye.

be free... 有空闲的

pick-up service 接送服务

balance payment 尾款
in advance 提前
set aside 搁置

be looking forward to doing sth. 期待做某事

 Notes

1. PDI (Pre Delivery Inspection): 出厂前检查。PDI 检查是一项售前检测证明,是新车在交车前必须通过的检查。

2. as much time as necessary: 尽可能多的时间。

3. I'm looking forward to seeing you! 期待您的到来!

Module Two Business English 商务英语

 Make your choice according to the situation A

	Questions	Answers
( )	1. When will Mr. Wang take his car?	A. Three hours.
( )	2. How long will it take for delivery?	B. On Sunday.
( )	3. What should Mr. Wang take for the delivery?	C. Four.
( )	4. How many parts are included in the delivery process?	D. ID card and enough money.
( )	5. What should salesman do before delivery?	E. The salesman should do the PDI and clean the car before delivery.

Situation B

What should be paid attention to in car acceptance?

> Mr. Wang comes to 4S store to take delivery of his car

(L—Mr. Lu, W—Mr. Wang)

L: Good morning, Mr. Wang! Welcome to our store to take delivery of your car.

W: Good morning, could you please introduce the delivery process for me?

L: Today we'll inspect the car before you take it.

W: What should be **paid attention to** in car acceptance?

L: Here is a checklist of what to look out before you take **acceptance**. You should pay attention to following parts: the outside and inside of the vehicle, **accessories**, etc. Which part do you want to inspect first?

W: Let's check the outside of the car.

L: Please walk around the car to check whether there are dents or scratches that might have occurred during transportation.

W: There are no defects on the **paint**, **trim** or glass.

L: Please check whether all the accessories are working properly, such as Bluetooth connectivity, the car radio, **indicators**, and **windscreen wipers**, etc.

W: I'm sure that all features and accessories that I contracted for are installed properly. Then what's the next part?

L: You should make sure you are **at ease** with all safety features such as rear-view camera, back-up sensors or tire pressure monitoring systems.

pay attention to 注意
acceptance 验收

accessories 配件

paint 油漆
trim 汽车装饰
indicator 指示器
windscreen wipers 风窗玻璃刮水器

at ease 安逸的

103

W: OK, let me adjust these equipment.

L: The new car will be filled with 1/4 of fuel in the gas tank.

W: Yes, there is still 1/4 of gasoline.

L: Now you've inspected the car thoroughly. If there is no damage on it, please sign these papers.

W: Yes, everything is alright. I'll sign on them.

 Notes

1. rear-view camera　　后视摄像头

   back-up sensors　　后备传感器

   tire pressure monitoring systems　　胎压监测系统

2. The new car will be filled with 1/4 of fuel in the gas tank.

   新车将在油箱中注满 1/4 的燃油。

 Make your choice according to the situation B

	Questions	Answers
(　)	1. What should be paid attention to in car acceptance?	A. 1/4 gas.
(　)	2. How to check the outside of the car?	B. Yes, I should.
(　)	3. What should be included when check the accessories?	C. The outside, inside and accessories, etc.
(　)	4. Should you make sure you are at ease with all safety features?	D. Walk around the car to check it.
(　)	5. How much fuel should be filled in the gas tank?	E. Bluetooth connectivity, the car radio, indicators, windscreen wipers, etc.

Module Two Business English 商务英语

Part Four: Practice

I. Complete these sentences with the given words.

> looking forward to, at ease, free, pay attention to, in advance, inspect, acceptance, walk around, sign, checklist

1. Are you _____ on Saturday?
2. You should prepare all the papers _____.
3. Please _____ its inside accessories.
4. I am _____ seeing you next time!
5. Which part do you want to _____ first?
6. You should feel _____ with your car security system.
7. You should check it carefully when you take your _____.
8. You should _____ the car when do your inspection.
9. Please _____ on it if you have no question.
10. Here is the _____ of the delivery.

II. Match the following Chinese with English expressions.

( )	1. 油箱	A. back-up sensors
( )	2. 风窗玻璃刮水器	B. gas tank
( )	3. 后备传感器	C. windscreen wipers
( )	4. 胎压监测系统	D. rear-view camera
( )	5. 后视摄像头	E. tire pressure monitoring systems

III. Put the following sentences into English.

1. 周六您有空吗？(be free...)
2. 如果没有损伤，请在文件上签字。(Please sign on...)
3. 欢迎来我们店里提车。(Welcome to...)
4. 您需要接送服务吗？(Do you need...)
5. 我应该预留多长时间提车。(How much time, set aside...)
6. 期待周日与您见面？(I'm looking forward to...)
7. 车辆验收时需要注意什么？(What should be paid attention to...)
8. 这是一份在车辆验收之前要注意的事项清单。(Here is the checklist...)

IV. Complete these tasks.

1. Play parts in the dialogues.

2. Make a dialogue according to the next situation: Supposing a customer comes to your store, he asks you many questions about how to inspect a car.

V. Self-check.

I learned:

(　) contract　　(　) dent　　(　) trim　　(　) instruction

(　) inspect　　(　) acceptance　　(　) checklist　　(　) confirm

(　) Bluetooth　　(　) prepare　　(　) damage　　(　) available

I can:

(　) make a delivery to customers.

(　) build a long-term good relationship with customers.

Module Two   Business English 商务英语

Lesson 7

Terms of Payment

  Learning Objectives:

Master the basic knowledge and skills	
➤ Language learning objective	Grasp the new words and useful expressions.
➤ Skill learning objectives	1. Be able to use different terms of payment in car purchasing. 2. Guide customers to choose the terms of payment.
Develop core competences of English	

➤ Know the culture and emotions conveyed by different texts on "Terms of Payment" topic.
➤ Know the differences in terms of payment between Chinese and Western.
➤ Develop the pragmatic competence in terms of payment scene.

Part One: Warming-up

Make your choice:

1. Which terms of payment do you know?
   (　) Cash.
   (　) Credit card.
   (　) Bank **Transfer**.
   (　) **Installment**.
   (　) Mobile pay.

What else?

transfer 转账
installment 分期付款

2. How should a salesman introduce the terms of payment?
   (　) Introduce it with examples.
   (　) Show some different **options**.

option 选项

107

clarify 阐明
policy 政策

( ) **Clarify** the related **policies**.
( ) Explain advantages and disadvantages clearly.

What else?
_____

suitable 适合的
reality 实际

3. How should a customer choose the **suitable** payment?
( ) According to his **reality**.
( ) According to his needs.

favor 喜好

( ) According to his **favor**.
( ) According to the policy.

What else?
_____

As a salesman, you should:

1. Know the advantages and disadvantages of every terms of payment.
2. Clarify the policy clearly and patiently to your customers.
3. Choose the terms of payment from customers' stand.
4. Accompany your customers to finish the payment **procedure**.

procedure 过程

Part Two: New Words and Useful Expressions

Ⅰ. New words.

pay	*v.* 付款
installment	*n.* 分期付款
decision	*n.* 决定
terms of payment	*n.* 付款方式
accept	*v.* 接受
cash	*n.* 现金
credit card	*n.* 信用卡
shipment	*n.* 装货
down installment	*n.* 首付款
prompt	*adj.* 及时的，迅速的

Ⅱ. Useful expressions.

1. Do you know our terms of payment?
2. Could you tell me which kind of payment you'll choose?
3. 2% discount for prompt payment.
4. Are you planning to pay in cash?
5. What are your payment terms?
6. If you pay in cash, we can offer you a discount.
7. Can I pay by bank transfer?
8. We accept payments in cash or by credit card only.
9. How much should I pay the first installment?
10. I will pay the first installment now.

1. 您知道我们的付款方式吗?
2. 您能告诉我您会选择哪种支付方式?
3. 立即付款打九八折。
4. 您要付现金吗?
5. 你们的付款方式如何?
6. 如果您付现金的话,可以给您折扣。
7. 我能通过银行汇款付款吗?
8. 我们只接受现金和信用卡付款。
9. 我首期付款要多少?
10. 我现在就付首期款。

Part Three: Situations

Situation A

I will pay by installments.

> Mr. White just talked about signing a contract with Lu Zhi. He decided to buy the model.

(L—Mr. Lu, W—Mr. White)

L: I'm very glad our business is going quite **smoothly.**

W: Me too, I love the model very much, 120,000 Yuan, White Aeolus AX7!

L: You have made a **wise** decision.

W: Now, I would like to talk about the terms of payment. Can I pay by **bank transfer**?

L: Sorry, I am afraid not. We accept payments in cash or by credit card only.

W: Oh, I don't think I have enough cash with me and I have no credit card.

L: We have installment payment which can help you.

W: I don't know much about payment by installment. Can you have a short **explanation**?

L: Of course. If you pay by installment, you should pay the first installment a week

---

smoothly 顺利地

wise 明智的
bank transfer 银行汇款

explanation 解释

before the shipment. The first installment is also called down payment, then you should pay the second installment one day before the shipment. Lastly you should pay the last installment when you get the car.

reasonable 合理的

W: That sound very **reasonable**. But how much should I pay the down installment?

L: It is 40,000 Yuan, 1/3 of the price.

W: That's great. I will pay the first installment now.

L: OK. This way, please.

 Notes

1. 分数表达法：分子用基数词，分母用序数词。若分子大于1，分母要加 s。
   E.g.: 1/3 读作：one third, 2/3 读作：two thirds, 4/5 读作：four fifths。
2. pay in cash：现金付款, pay by credit card：信用卡付款, pay by installment：分期付款。

Make your choice according to situation A.

	Questions	Answers
( )	1. Did Mr. White decide to buy the car?	A. Because he didn't have enough cash with him and had no credit card.
( )	2. Which terms of payment does Mr. White want to choose at the beginning?	B. Yes, he did.
( )	3. Why didn't Mr. White choose to pay in cash or by credit card?	C. Yes, it is.
( )	4. Is the first installment equal to the down payment?	D. At last, he would pay by installment.
( )	5. Which terms of payment did Mr. White choose at last?	E. He wanted to pay by the bank transfer.

Situation B

Do you know our terms of payment?

> Lu Zhi just had a pleasant talk with Mrs. Green who has decided to buy a car from him.

(L—Mr. Lu, G—Mrs. Green)

L: It's so pleasant to cooperate with a lady like you.
G: I think it's because of **predestination**, I buy a new car from you.
L: Yes, it's **marvelous**. Do you know our terms of payment?
G: No. What are they?
L: We accept both credit card and cash. What's more, you can pay by installment.
G: Is there any difference between the payment by credit card and by installment?
L: Yes, if you pay by credit card or cash, we will offer you 2% discount for prompt payment, but **net** for payment by installments.
G: Oh, I see.
L: So... Are you planning to pay by credit card?
G: Yes, that's right.
L: In that case we can offer you 2% discount.
G: Good. I am glad to hear it.

 Notes

1. 百分比表达法：2%读作 two percent，90%读作 ninety percent。
2. cooperate with   与……合作
   e.g.: I'm glad to cooperate with you. 很高兴和你合作。We will cooperate with the bank. 我们将与银行合作。
3. difference between... and...   与……之间有不同
   e.g.: Is there any difference between cash and credit card? 使用现金和信用卡有什么不同吗？
4. in that case   如果是那样的话

Make your choice according to situation B.

	Questions	Answers
( )	1. Did Mrs. Green know the terms of payment?	A. Both cash and credit card.
( )	2. Which terms of payment did they accept?	B. Yes, they did.
( )	3. Did they accept the payment by installment?	C. She decided to pay by credit card.
( )	4. Was there any discount for prompt payment?	D. No, she didn't.
( )	5. Which term of payment did Mrs. Green decide to pay by?	E. Yes, they would offer 2% discount.

Part Four: Practice

Ⅰ. Complete these sentences with the given words in the box.

> choose, reasonable, accept, decision, discount, offer, cooperate, shipment, pay, difference

1. We _____ payments in cash or by credit card only.
2. We will _____ you 2% discount for prompt payment.
3. You have made a wise _____.
4. It's so pleasant to _____ with a lady like you.
5. Could you tell me which kind of payment you'll _____.
6. I will _____ by installment.
7. Is there any _____ between the payment by credit card and by installment?
8. That sounds _____.
9. Is there any _____ for the payment by installment?
10. If you pay by installment, you should pay the first installment a week before the _____.

Ⅱ. Write the following in English.

1/3	6/7	5%	90%
4/5	3/5	20%	100%

III. Put the words or expressions into chinese.

1. pay
2. payment
3. terms of payment
4. pay in cash
5. pay by credit card
6. pay by installment
7. pay the down installment
8. pay by bank transfer

IV. Complete the following tasks.

1. Play the parts in the dialogues.
2. Make a dialogue according to the next situation: Supposing a rich customer decides to buy your car. Now introduce the terms of payment for him, please.

V. Self-check.

I learned:

( ) pay   ( ) installment   ( ) cash   ( ) credit
( ) prompt   ( ) wise   ( ) smoothly   ( ) payment
( ) reasonable   ( ) smoothly   ( ) discount   ( ) active

I can:

( ) tell terms of payment according to the policies.
( ) know about the different terms of payment.
( ) guide customers to choose the terms of payment.

 Lesson 8

Settling Complaints

Learning Objectives:

Master the basic knowledge and skills	
➢ Language learning objective	Grasp the new words and useful expressions.
➢ Skill learning objectives	1. Be able to understand the different ways to make complaints. 2. Settle complaints in time.
Develop core competences of English	

➢ Know the culture and emotions conveyed by different texts on "Settling Complaints" topic.
➢ Know the differences between Chinese and Western thinking in English expression.
➢ Develop the pragmatic competence in settling complaints scene.

Part One: Warming-up

 Make your choice:

1. If you are a customer, how will you make your complaint?
   (　) There is something wrong with my...
   (　) I was extremely disappointed with your service.
   (　) I want to complain about...
   (　) I wish you can pay attention to...

   What else?

2. If you are a clerk, how will you settle complaints?
   (　) Do not quarrel with customers.
   (　) Try my best to **solve** the problems for customers.
   (　) Express my apologizes to customers at first.

solve 解决

( ) Interrupt customers when they are making complaints.

What else?

_____

3. If you are a clerk, how should you **treat with** the customer who is **unreasonable** and hard to **deal with**?

( ) Show my regrets to him.
( ) Ask my manager to solve his problem.
( ) Find an excuse to end the talk with him.
( ) Talk something else with him friendly.

What else?

_____

treat with 应付
unreasonable 不讲理的
deal with 处理

 When you set complaints, you should:

1. Know your customers' needs and requirements.
2. Never be angry with your customers.
3. Deal with their complaints quickly.
4. Be aware of protecting customers' right.

Part Two: New Words and Useful Expressions

Ⅰ. New words.

quality	*n.* 质量
garage	*n.* 修理厂
repair	*v.* 修理
check	*v.* 检查
test	*v.* 测试
mechanic	*n.* 技术工人
escape	*v.* 逃避
guarantee	*v.* 保证
unpleasant	*adj.* 不愉快的
order	*v.* 订购

examine	*v.* 检查，调试
signal	*n.* 信号
connection	*n.* 接头
ridiculous	*adj.* 可笑的，荒唐的

Ⅱ. Useful expressions.

1. I have to make a complaint with your company.
2. I'm sorry to hear that.
3. There is something wrong with...
4. I'll check it and send a repairman to your side.
5. Can I return this?
6. Sorry, we don't offer returns.
7. If we were at fault, we should make good your loss.
8. I want to talk to the manager.
9. What would you like me to do to fix the situation?
10. Your claim is unreasonable.

1. 我不得不向你公司投诉。
2. 听到此事我很抱歉。
3. ……坏了。
4. 我会查一下并派维修人员上门。
5. 我可以退货吗？
6. 抱歉，我们不提供退货。
7. 如果我方过错，我们将赔偿您的损失。
8. 我想和你们经理谈。
9. 您想要我怎样做来挽救？
10. 您的要求不合理。

Part Three: Situations

Situation A

I have to make a complaint…

Anna's new car has broken down. She is calling to make a complaint.

(L—Mr. Lu, A—Anna)

L: Thank you for calling JiHeng Auto Sales Company. How can I help you?

A: I have to **make a complaint** with your company. I have always been able to **rely on** the high quality of your cars and your service. But I'm afraid this time I have to **change my mind**.

L: I'm sorry to hear that. However, why **on earth**?

A: I just **picked up** my Aeolus S30 from your garage, and the same problem come again.

make a complaint 投诉
rely on 信赖
change my mind 改变想法
on earth 究竟
pick up 拿到

Module Two Business English 商务英语

L: Again? However, how can that be? Every car is checked before being **sent out**.

A: Yes. That's what I want to ask you.

L: Maybe it escaped the test.

A: You know, I just bought it three months ago.

L: Oh, I'm sorry to hear that.

A: I had a new transmission put in this months. However, it **broke down** again. The car is a real lemon and I've already spent a lot of money in repairing it.

L: I will send our mechanic to get your car back and **check it over** right now. If there is something wrong with the new transmission, we'll provide another one for you **for free**. Is that OK?

A: OK. Thank you!

L: You are welcome. And I'll **get on to** our **inspection department** and let them guarantee the quality.

send out 发出

break down 坏了

check over 仔细检查

for free 免费
get on to 联系
inspection 检验
department 部门

 Notes

1. A real lemon   次品
2. I just picked up my Aeolus S30 from your garage. 我刚把我的风神 S30 从修理厂开回来。
3. I had a new transmission put in this morning. 我今天早上才换了新的变速器。

 Make your choice according to situation A.

Questions	Answers
(　) 1. Why did Anna complain?	A. Serve the customer with heart and soul.
(　) 2. How did Mr. Lu settle the complaints?	B. Because her new car has broke down again.
(　) 3. Did Mr. Lu agree to provide a new transmission for Anna?	C. Yes, if it is broken.
(　) 4. Why did Mr. Lu say the last sentence?	D. Yes, she did.
(　) 5. Did Anna satisfy the response?	E. Because he wanted to save the company fame.

Situation B

I'm sorry to hear that.

Mr. Black bought a new car and ordered a set of wheel alignment from Lu Zhi. Now he is making a complaint.

(L—Mr. Lu, B—Mr. Black)

L: Good morning. This is JiHeng Auto Sales Company. May I help you?

B: Yes. I'm afraid I have to make a complaint with your company. It's a most unpleasant thing.

L: Oh, I'm sorry to hear that. What is it about?

B: I ordered **a set of wheel alignment the other day**. When I received and examined them one by one, I found that there was something wrong with the computer because it couldn't give out any signal.

L: Did you check the connection?

B: Yes, I did. No problem there.

L: That's strange. I'll check it and send a mechanic to your side at once.

B: Can I return this?

L: Sorry, we don't offer returns. If we **were at fault**, we should **make good** your loss. I am sure everything is all right with that shipment.

B: What? That's ridiculous! I want to talk to the manager.

L: Hold on, please. I'll **put you through**.

a set of 一套
wheel alignment 四轮定位仪
the other day 前几天

be at fault 有过错
make good 补偿

put through 接通

Make your choice according to situation B.

( )	Questions	Answers
( )	1. What did Mr. Black order?	A. Because he wanted to return that.
( )	2. What's wrong with the wheel alignment?	B. No, he didn't.
( )	3. Did Mr. Lu agree Mr. Black to talk to the manager?	C. Yes, he was.
( )	4. Why did Mr. Black want to talk to the manager at last?	D. There was no signal on the screen.
( )	5. Was Mr. Black satisfy with the response?	E. He ordered a set of wheel alignment.

Part Four: Practice

I. Complete these sentences with the words and phrases in the box.

> make a complaint, examine, rely on, guarantee, escape, put you through, pick up, check, unpleasant, make good

1. Maybe it _____ the examination.
2. We have to _____ with your company.
3. I just _____ my Accord from your garage.
4. Hold on, please. I'll _____.
5. I will _____ those transmissions one by one.
6. We have always been able to _____ the high quality of your cars.
7. Did you _____ the connection?
8. We will _____ our quality.
9. If we were at fault, we should _____ your loss.
10. I'm sorry, it's a most _____ thing.

II. Match the following Chinese with English expressions.

(　)	1. 四轮定位仪	A. make good your loss
(　)	2. 变速器	B. transmission
(　)	3. 投诉	C. wheel alignment
(　)	4. 处理投诉	D. settle complaints
(　)	5. 赔偿损失	E. make a complaint

III. Put the following sentences into English.

1. 我要投诉你们公司。(make a complaint...)
2. 您的车出了什么故障？(What's wrong with...)
3. 我的车坏了。(break down...)
4. 我们会免费为您更换新的变速器。(for free)
5. 职员应该如何处理投诉？(How does a clerk...)
6. 我前几天才订购的新车。(order)

IV. Complete the following tasks.

1. Play the parts in the dialogues.

2. Make a dialogue according to the next situation: John is settling complaints, his customer Tom finds there is the painting problem with his new car.

V. Self-check.

I learned:

( ) quality ( ) garage ( ) repair ( ) mechanic
( ) regret ( ) complaint ( ) settle ( ) escape
( ) check ( ) examine

I can:

( ) make a complaint.
( ) settle complaints.

Module Two　Business English 商务英语

Lesson 9

Customer Feedback

Learning Objectives:

Master the basic knowledge and skills	
➢ Language learning objective	Grasp the new words and useful expressions.
➢ Skill learning objectives	1. Be able to use standardized service language to make a feedback call. 2. Ask for suggestions and make a suggestion.
Develop core competences of English	
➢ Know the culture and emotions conveyed by different texts on "Customer Feedback" topic. ➢ Know the differences between Chinese and Western thinking in English expression. ➢ Develop the pragmatic competence in customer feedback scene.	

Part One: Warming-up

Make your choice:

1. If a customer bought a car from your company, how should you make a **feedback call**?

    (　) Ask if the car has experienced **unexpected** situations during driving.

    (　) Ask if the customer needs help or service from my company.

    (　) Answer all questions for the customer professionally.

    (　) Give some suggestions on car **maintenance** to customers.

    What else?

2. If a customer has his car repaired in your company, how should you make a feedback call?

    (　) Ask customers whether they **are satisfied with** the last repair service.

    (　) Ask whether the car has experienced any conditions after the maintenance.

feedback 反馈

unexpected 出乎意料

maintenance 维修

be satisfied with
对……满意

(   ) Try to win the trust and satisfaction.

(   ) Make some explanations based on what the customer was worried about.

_____

3. If your customer **is not satisfied with** your car or your maintenance, what will you do?

(   ) Say "I'm very sorry".

(   ) Write down the information.

(   ) Say nothing and go away.

(   ) Promise to send the suggestions to the manager.

_____

As a salesman, you should:

1. Make a feedback call regularly.
2. Treat customers **fairly** and **reasonably**.
3. Never **ignore** customer's feedback.
4. Record every detail of customer's feedback.

fairly 公平的
reasonably 合理地
ignore 忽略

Part Two: New Words and Useful Expressions

I. New words.

cause	*v.* 引起
room	*n.* 空间
market research	*n.* 市场调查
report	*v.* 报告
limited	*adj.* 有限的
further	*adv.* 进一步
appreciate	*v.* 感谢
necessary	*adj.* 必要的
suggestion	*n.* 建议
cooperation	*n.* 合作

Module Two Business English 商务英语

II. Useful expressions.

1. I'm calling to know whether everything is going well with your car.	1. 我打电话想知道您的车现在是否运行良好。
2. Is everything going well with your car?	2. 您的车用得可好?
3. It works well after being repaired.	3. 自从修过之后，它很好。
4. I feel the room of the car is so limited that I always can't move freely in it.	4. 我觉得车的空间太小，以至于我不能在里面自由移动。
5. I really appreciate your buying our car.	5. 十分感谢您购买我们的汽车。
6. Have you got used to driving our car?	6. 驾驶我们的车习惯吗?
7. It's necessary for us to know them well.	7. 我们有必要了解这些。
8. We are ready for help at any time.	8. 我们随时为您效劳。
9. The standard safety features are well equipped.	9. 安全设施配备很好。
10. Thank you for your cooperation.	10. 感谢您的合作。

Part Three: Situations

Situation A

Has everything gone well with your car?

> Mr. Lu is calling Mr. Black whose car was repaired last week.

(L—Mr. Lu, B—Mr. Black)

L: Hello, this is JiHeng Auto Sales Company. Is that Mr. Black?

B: Yes, this is.

L: I'm calling to know whether everything is going well with your car.

B: Thanks a lot. It works well after being repaired.

L: I'm very happy to hear that and I do hope the problem didn't cause you much **inconvenience**.

B: Thank you very much for your good service. I'm sure your company will be making more money.

L: It is always our **policy** to give **satisfactory** services to our customers. Now I want to do a market research and it will help us a lot. What do you think of the car?

B: I feel the room of the car is so limited that I always can't move freely in it. And

inconvenience 不方便

policy 政策
satisfactory 满意

warm-hearted 热情的

the painting is not very good.

L：It's a good suggestion. I will report it to the manager. What's more?

B：Oh, no more.

L：Thank you for your **warm-hearted** reply.

B：It's just my own opinion.

L：We'll go into it further. Thank you for your suggestions. Bye-bye!

B：Bye!

 Notes

1. It works well after being repaired. 车辆自从修过之后，工作良好。being repaired 是动名词的被动形式。

2. I do hope the problem didn't cause you much inconvenience. 衷心希望这次修理没有给您带来不便。do 放在谓语动词前表强调。

3. I feel the room of the car is so limited that I always can't move freely in it. 我认为车的空间太小，以至于总是不能在里面自由移动。So...that...：如此……以至于……，引导结果状语从句。

Make your choice according to situation A.

	Questions	Answers
(　)	1. Who is Mr. Lu calling?	A. Yes, it has.
(　)	2. Does the car work well?	B. Mr. Black.
(　)	3. Has the car been repaired before?	C. No, he isn't.
(　)	4. Is Mr. Black satisfied with the car?	D. No, he doesn't.
(　)	5. Does Mr. Black answer the question with angry?	E. Yes, it does.

Situation B

We are ready for help anytime.

Mr. Hunter has already bought a car. Mr. Lu is telephoning how things are going.

(L—Mr. Lu, H—Mr. Hunter)

L：Hello, this is Lu Zhi calling from JiHeng Auto Sales Company. Could I speak to Mr. Hunter who bought Aeolus AX7 eight weeks ago.

H：Yes, speaking.

Module Two　Business English　商务英语

L：Mr. Hunter, I really appreciate your buying our car. May I take you a few minutes to ask you a few questions?

H：OK.

L：Thank you. How many kilometers has your car traveled now?

H：About 1,700 kilometers.

L：Is everything going well with your car?

H：Yes. In general, the car is very **powerful** and I am quite satisfied.

L：What do you think of the **interior**?

H：It's **spacious**, comfortable, and **functional**. The **dashboard** is clear and intelligent, and **operating devices** are within the reach.

L：What do you think of the performance?

H：The fuel consumption is not very high, the standard safety **feature**s are well **equipped**. It's multi-touch central control screen, 5G wireless network, and on-board artificial intelligence system are cool.

L：Thank you for your **affirmation**. Is there anything **discontent**?

H：The paint workmanship is just so-so and the chassis is not high enough.

L：Thank you very much for your feedback, and we will try to improve them. By the way, the car needs first maintenance when driving 2,500 kilometers. You need to replace engine oil, engine filter and gear oil and make a free inspection of the whole car.

H：OK.

L：And if you have any questions or car failures, please call 87443578. We are ready for help at any time. Thank you for your cooperation. Goodbye.

H：Goodbye.

interior 内饰
spacious 宽敞的
functional 实用的
dashboard 仪表盘
operating devices 操纵装置
performance 性能
consumption 消耗
standard 标准的
feature 设施
equip 配备
affirmation 肯定
discontent 不满意

Notes

1. multi-touch central control screen　多点触摸中控屏
2. 5G wireless network　5G 无线网络
3. on-board artificial intelligence system　车载人工智能系统

Make your choice according to situation B.

	Questions	Answers
(　)	1. Who is Mr. Lu calling?	A. Yes, he has.
(　)	2. Has Mr. Hunter bought the car?	B. Yes, he is.
(　)	3. Can Mr. Hunter drive the car?	C. Yes. It does.

	Questions	Answers
( )	4. Is Mr. Hunter satisfied with the car?	D. Mr. Hunter.
( )	5. Does the company offer the service at any time?	E. Yes, he can.

Part Four: Practice

Ⅰ. Complete these sentences with the words and phrases in the box.

> thank…for, so…that, being repaired, after all, gone well with, got used to, appreciate, cause, necessary

1. Have you _____ driving our car?
2. I feel the room of the car is _____ limited _____ I always can't move freely in it.
3. I really _____ you buying our car.
4. It works well after _____.
5. I'm calling to know whether everything has _____ your car.
6. _____, safety is the first.
7. _____ you very much _____ your good service.
8. It's _____ for us to know them well.
9. I do hope the problem didn't _____ you much inconvenience.

Ⅱ. Match the following Chinese with English expressions.

( )	1. 合作	A. room
( )	2. 路况	B. market research
( )	3. 感谢	C. road condition
( )	4. 市场调查	D. appreciate
( )	5. 空间	E. cooperation

Ⅲ. Put the following words in order.

1. 开快车是危险的。(dangerous, is, to drive fast, it)

   _____

2. 有必要了解交通规则。(is, know, the traffic regulations, it, necessary to)

   _____

3. 学生们学好英语是重要的。(for the students, it, important, is, to learn English well.)

_____

4. 这个盒子太重了,那个男孩拿不动。(so heavy, this box, that boy, is, that, carry it, can't)

_____

5. 道路太滑,以至于他不得不挂一档行驶。(so slippery, drive the car, the road, had to, was, he, that, at first gear)

_____

Ⅳ. Complete these tasks.

1. Play the parts in the dialogues.
2. Make a dialogue according to the next situation: Supposing a doctor bought a car from your 4S Store, now you are making a feedback call.

Ⅴ. Self-check.

I learned:

( ) feedback   ( ) research   ( ) limited   ( ) appreciate
( ) necessary   ( ) cooperation   ( ) policy   ( ) satisfactory
( ) Warm-hearted   ( ) discontent   ( ) further   ( ) cause

I can:

( ) make a call for feedback.
( ) ask for suggestions.
( ) deal with suggestions.

Lesson 10

Maintenance Reception

Learning Objectives:

Master the basic knowledge and skills	
➢ Language learning objective	Grasp the new words and useful expressions.
➢ Skill learning objective	1. Be able to receive customers and collect the useful information when customers need vehicle maintenance. 2. Know the process of vehicle maintenance.
Develop core competences of English	

➢ Know the culture and emotions conveyed by different texts on "Maintenance Reception" topic.
➢ Know the differences between Chinese and Western thinking in English expression.
➢ Develop the pragmatic competence in maintenance reception scene.

Part One: Warming-up

Make your choice:

1. If you are a salesman of Audi 4S store, how will you begin talks with customers?
   (　) Hello, this is Audi 4S store. How can I help you?
   (　) Good morning. What can I do for you?
   (　) Welcome to our 4S store. I'm Lucy, What do you need, sir?
   (　) If you have any problems, please let me know.

   What else?

2. If you are a salesman of Audi 4S store, how will you receive a customer?
   (　) Record the problem of his vehicle.
   (　) Note the basic information of the customer.

Module Two   Business English 商务英语

(　　) Write down the customer's maintenance **requirements**.
(　　) **Make an appointment** of the maintenance time.

What else?
_____

requirement 需求
make an appointment 预约

3. What should you pay attention to when you make maintenance reception?
(　　) Make an appointment with the customer **in advance**.
(　　) Greeting with the customer with smile.
(　　) **Confirm** and note requirements of the customer.
(　　) Talk with someone else when you receive a customer.

What else?
_____

in advance 提前

confirm 确认

  As a desk clerk, you should：

1. Answer questions **professionally**.
2. Write down useful information about car models, problems, date of purchasing.
3. Check the imformation clearly and carefully.
4. Submit the imformation to **inventory management department**.

professionally 专业地
inventory 仓库
management 管理
department 部门

Part Two：New Words and Useful Expressions

Ⅰ. New words.

describe	***v.*** 描述
detail	***n.*** 细节，详情
failure	***n.*** 故障，失败
seldom	***adv.*** 很少
crash	***n. & v.*** 碰撞，事故
arrange	***v.*** 安排
arrival	***n.*** 到达
depend	***v.*** 依靠，取决于
fetch	***v.*** 取回
paperwork	***n.*** 文书工作
costs	***n.*** 费用

129

Ⅱ. Useful expressions.

1. How can I help you?
2. What's the matter with your car?
3. Could you please describe the problem in detail?
4. Our mechanic will reach you in... minutes.
5. Which year and model is it?
6. We will call you in time.
7. We'll try our best.
8. Please fill the paperwork and leave your telephone number to us.
9. My car needs servicing.
10. Can I get my car back tomorrow?

1. 能为您效劳吗?
2. 您的车怎么了?
3. 您能详细描述一下车辆的问题吗?
4. 我们的技工将在……分钟内赶到。
5. 您的车是哪年的,什么款?
6. 我们会及时与您联系的。
7. 我们会尽力的。
8. 请填张表并给我们留下您的电话号码。
9. 我的车子要维修。
10. 我能明天取回我的车吗?

Part Three：Situations

Situation A

My car has broken down.

Mr. Bush's car has broken down. He is calling the JiHeng Auto Garage for help. Wang——a desk clerk, answers the phone.

（W—Wang，B—Mr. Bush）

W：Good morning. This is JiHeng Auto Garage. How can I help you?

B：Yes. I need your help because my car has broken down.

W：Oh. I'm sorry to hear that. Could you please describe it **in detail**?

B：I think it might be an engine failure, but I'm not quite sure. And it doesn't seem to run right. I mean every time I **start** it **up**, the engine runs for a minute **or so**, **sputters** like it isn't getting enough gas, and then dies.

W：Which year and model is it?

B：It's a 2019 model Toyota RV 2.0AT.

W：**Generally speaking**, this kind of car seldom needs repairing. Didn't you have a crash?

B：Yes. I drove it into a **lamp post**. Can you arrange a mechanic to repair it?

W：No problem. Please tell me your name, place and mobile phone number.

in detail 详细地

start up 起动
or so 大约
sputter 噼啪声

generally speaking 一般说来

lamp post 灯柱

B: All right. I am Fed Bush. My number is 13312345678 and I am on the street near the front gate of Zhong Shan Park. I'm **looking forward to** your arrival.

W: I see. Our mechanic will reach you in 20 minutes. Try to keep you and your car safe. See you.

B: Thank you.

W: That's all right. Bye.

look forward to 期待

 Notes

1. needs repairing 需要维修= needs to be repaired
2. It's a 2019 model Toyota RV 2.0MT: 它是2019年的丰田2.0升自动档休闲车型。

 Make your choice according to situation A.

	Questions	Answers
( )	1. Why did Mr. Bush call the garage?	A. Yes, he will.
( )	2. Did Mr. Bush have a car crash?	B. Because his car has broken down.
( )	3. Why does Wang ask the year and model?	C. Because it will be very helpful for a mechanic to judge the problem.
( )	4. Why must Wang ask Mr. Bush about the phone number and place?	D. Because the mechanic will connect with him.
( )	5. Will Mr. Bush wait for the mechanic?	E. Yes, he did.

Situation B

My car needs repairing.

> Mrs. Green gets to JiHeng Auto Garage. Wang—a desk clerk, receives him.

(W—Wang, G—Mrs. Green)

W: Good morning, Madam. May I help you?

G: Yes, my car needs repairing. Can I get it done here?

W: Certainly, Madam. What's the matter with your car?

G: I heard the bang-ping noise from my car three days ago.

Automobile Business English 汽车商务英语 第3版

W: Oh, really? Is it a big bang or a small bang?

G: A small bang I think, but it seems to be getting a little louder.

W: Oh? We'll check it for you.

G: Can I get my car back tomorrow?

W: We'll **try our best**. But it **depends on** what the noise problem is. I'll give you a call when we know the problem. Please **fill the paperwork** and leave your telephone number to us. We will call you in time.

G: OK.

(The next day, Mrs. Green wants to fetch her car. She is dialing...)

W: Hello, JiHeng Auto Garage.

G: Hello, this is Tina Green. I sent my car to your garage yesterday. I'd like to know if I could fetch my car this afternoon.

W: Wait a moment, please. I will check it for you.

G: OK, thank you.

W: Eh... Mrs. Green, we are planning to call you right now. There is something wrong with the **shock absorber** and it needs to be replaced.

G: So...?

W: Don't worry. Our mechanic is replacing a new shock absorber for you.

G: Oh, it's so good. Can I get my car back this afternoon?

W: No problem.

G: By the way, what about the costs?

W: 280 RMB.

G: Thank you. See you this afternoon.

W: See you.

try one's best 尽力
depend on 依据
fill paperwork 填表登记

shock absorber 减振器

Notes

1. Can I get it done here? 能在这里维修吗？get sth. done 让某物被……

2. It seems to be getting a litter louder. 它好像变得更响了。it seems to be... 它似乎/好像……

Module Two Business English 商务英语

 Make your choice according to situation B.

	Questions	Answers
( )	1. Is there a ping-pong noise from Mrs. Green's car?	A. Shock absorber goes badly.
( )	2. What's wrong with her car on earth?	B. Yes, she can.
( )	3. Can Mrs. Green fetch her car this afternoon?	C. Yes, there is.
( )	4. How much will Mrs. Green pay for the maintenance?	D. Yes, she does.
( )	5. Does Mrs. Green satisfy the service?	E. 280 RMB

Part Four: Practice

I. Complete these sentences with the words and phrases in the box.

> fetch, start it up, needs, leave, depends on, fill, describe, costs, seems to, looking forward to, broken down

1. Could you please _____ it in detail?
2. How much should I pay for the _____?
3. We are _____ your arrival.
4. Every time when I _____, it runs for a while and then dies.
5. The shock absorber _____ to be replaced.
6. The noise _____ be getting a little louder.
7. Please _____ a paperwork and _____ your telephone number to us.
8. I need your help because my car has _____.
9. The time _____ what the noise problem is?
10. The next day, Mrs Green wants to _____ her car.

II. Match the following Chinese with English expressions.

( )	1. 填表登记	A. start up
( )	2. 减振器	B. costs
( )	3. 发动机故障	C. engine failure
( )	4. 起动	D. fill a paperwork
( )	5. 费用	E. shock absorber

Ⅲ. Put the following sentences into English.

1. 我的车辆需要维修。(need doing...)
2. 车辆熄火了。(die)
3. 这辆车无法起动。(start up)
4. 你的车出了什么故障？(What's the matter/wrong...)
5. 今天能取车吗？(fetch...)
6. 我们会及时联系您的。(call)

Ⅳ. Complete the following tasks.

1. Play the parts in the dialogues.
2. Make a dialogue according to the next situation: Supposing you are servicing at the front desk, a customer comes in. She wants to do a basic maintenance for her car.

Ⅴ. Self-check.

I learned:

(　) describe　　(　) detail　　(　) seldom　　(　) collect
(　) crash　　　(　) arrival　　(　) fetch　　　(　) paperwork
(　) failure　　 (　) mechanic

I can:

(　) collect the useful information.
(　) receive a customer on phone.
(　) begin talks.

Module Two Business English 商务英语

Lesson 11

Vehicle Maintenance

  Learning Objectives：

Master the basic knowledge and skills	
➤ Language learning objective	Grasp the new words and useful expressions.
➤ Skill learning objectives	1. Be able to collect the useful information of maintenance requirements. 2. Give some suggestions on vehicle maintenance.
Develop core competences of English	

➤ Know the culture and emotions conveyed by different texts on "Vehicle Maintenance" topic.
➤ Know the differences between Chinese and Western thinking in English expression.
➤ Develop the pragmatic competence in vehicle maintenance scene.

Part One：Warming-up

Make your choice：

1. If you are a **mechanic**, what should you pay attention to when you serve a customer outside?
(   ) Collect the breakdown information.
(   ) Arrive in time.
(   ) Call him to make sure the problem.
(   ) Check the problem carefully.
(   ) Never forget to check at the **warranty**.

> What else?

mechanic 维修师

warranty 保修单

2. If you are a customer, what will you do when the mechanic is fixing your car outside?
(   ) **Describe** the problem of my car in detail.

describe 描述

135

repair process 维修过程

( ) Watch the **repair process** carefully.
( ) Try to give him a hand when necessary.
( ) Show my gratitude to the mechanic.

 What else?

3. If you are a mechanic, what should you do when you repair a car in your garage?

customer lounge 顾客休息厅
wash and wax 清洗和打蜡

( ) Check the problems as soon as possible.
( ) Let the customer wait in **customer lounge**.
( ) Suggest the customer to **wash and wax** his car when it's very dirty.
( ) Explain customer's problems in detail.

 What else?

 As a mechanic, you should：

1. Get to know the condition at first.
2. **Analyze** the **breakdown** quickly.
3. Check and solve the breakdown **professionally**.
4. Show how to do the car maintenance in daily life.

analyze 分析
breakdown 故障
professionally 专业地

Part Two：New Words and Useful Expressions

Ⅰ. New words.

squeal	*v.* 尖叫
repair	*v.* 修理
parts	*n.* 零部件
repairs	*n.* 修理费
basic	*adj.* 基础的
maintenance	*n.* 维护
wax	*v.* 打蜡
surface	*n.* 表面
scratch	*v.* 擦伤

Module Two Business English 商务英语

sponge	*n.*	海绵
rag	*n.*	布块
beautify	*v.*	美化
dry	*v.*	弄干
rub	*v.*	擦
replace	*v.*	替换，更换
directions	*n.*	说明书

Ⅱ. Useful expressions.

1. What's wrong with the car?
2. Do you have... (a spare tire)?
3. Nothing serious. I can repair it right now.
4. Would you like to have your car washed and waxed?
5. I'd like to have a basic maintenance.
6. We have to pull your car back to the garage.
7. Can I have a look at your warranty certificate?
8. We have to charge for the parts.
9. Your warranty has come to an end.
10. If anything is wrong with your car, please call us and we are at your service.

1. 这车怎么了。
2. 您有……（备用轮胎）吗？
3. 没什么大问题，我马上就可以修好。
4. 您的车要清洗打蜡吗？
5. 我想做一个基础维护。
6. 我们得把您的车拖回修理厂。
7. 能看一下您的保修单吗？
8. 我们要收取零件费。
9. 你的保修单过期了。
10. 如果您的车再出故障请给我们打电话，我们将随时为您服务。

Part Three: Situations

Situation A

You've finally arrived.

> Mr. Black just called the garage for help. Now he is waiting for the mechanic.

(B—Mr. Black, M—Mechanic)

B: You've finally arrived.
M: What's wrong with the car?

drive at a low speed 低速驾驶	B: I think something is wrong with my brake, because when I **drive** my car **at a low speed**, braking as needed, the brake squeals.
the brake pads 制动片	M: Let me have a look... Oh, **the brake pads** went dead.
	B: Really?
	M: Yes, we have to pull your car back to the garage to repair it.
	B: No problem.
	(An hour past, the car was pulled to the garage and replaced a new brake pad.)
	M: It's OK now, you can try driving your car for a while.
warranty certificate 保修卡	B: OK... Oh, the squeals have gone. Thank you.
	M: You are welcome. Can I have a look at your **warranty certificate**?
come to an end 过期了	B: Yes, of course. Here you are.
charge for 收……费	M: Well, your warranty **has come to an end**. We have to **charge for** the parts.
maintaining sheet 维修单	B: That's all right.
the front desk 前台	M: Please sign your name here, and take **maintaining sheet** to **the front desk** and pay for repairs.
	B: Thank you for coming here in time.
	M: If anything is wrong with your car, please call us and we are at your service.
	B: Thanks again.
	M: My pleasure.

 Notes

1. braking as needed：由于需要而制动时。
2. the brake pads went dead：制动片坏了。
3. We are at your service. 我们随时为您效劳。

 Make your choice according to situation A.

	Questions	Answers
( )	1. What's wrong with Mr. Black's car?	A. No, it isn't. It's in the garage.
( )	2. Why does the repairman ask for looking at the warranty certificate?	B. Because if the warranty comes to an end, they must charge for the parts.
( )	3. Is his car repaired on the road?	C. Yes, it has.
( )	4. Why does the brake of his car squeal?	D. Because the brake pads went dead.
( )	5. Has the warranty certificate come to an end?	E. When he drive his car at low speed, braking as needed, the brake squeals.

Module Two   Business English 商务英语

Situation B

Would you like to have it washed and waxed?

> Tom drives his car to auto-garage for maintenance and asks some common questions about maintaining a new car.

(W—Wang, T—Tom)

W: How are you, sir? What can I do for you?

T: I'd like to have a five-thousand-kilometer basic maintenance.

W: No problem. Please take a rest in our customer lounge. I'll begin right away.

T: Thank you.

(Half an hour later.)

W: Sir, the maintenance for your car has been finished. But your car is very dirty, would you like to have it washed and waxed?

T: All right. By the way, can you show me the way to wash and wax my car?

W: First of all, **flush away** the dust and the sand on the surface of the car with water. In this way the car won't be scratched.

flush away 冲洗去

T: What should I use to wash it? How should I wash it?

W: Only use a clean sponge and **car detergent** to wash the body. Wash it up and down at first, and then backward and forward. The wheels are washed last.

car detergent 汽车清洗剂

T: With what to dry it?

W: With a **special polish rag**. If you use a common rag, its **fluff** will **stick to** the surface.

special polish rag 特殊的抛光布
fluff 绒毛
stick to 附着

T: After that, what should I do next?

W: Use different kinds of waxes for beautifying its body and leather seats. Body waxes **are divided into** two kinds: hard wax and soft wax. **Generally speaking**, hard wax lasts longer.

be divided into 分为
generally speaking 一般说来

T: When waxing, what do I need to pay special attention to?

W: Make sure no dust is on the surface. **For fear of** wasting too much wax, **a thin layer** is OK.

for fear of 为避免
a thin layer 薄薄一层

T: Do I need to wait until the wax is dry before I rub it clean with the sponge.

W: Certainly. **As a matter of fact**, you just use them **according to** the directions.

as a matter of fact 事实上
according to 按照，根据

T: Thank you very much.

Notes

1. a five-thousand-kilometer basic maintenance：5000km 基础维护。
2. Wash it up and down at first, and then backward and forward. 首先上下洗，然后前后洗。
3. For fear of wasting too much wax, a thin layer is OK. 为避免浪费过多的蜡，薄薄一层就可以了。

 Make your choice according to situation B.

	Questions	Answers
( )	1. What does Tom want to do for his car at the very beginning?	A. A clean sponge and car detergent.
( )	2. What is used to wash a car?	B. Yes. Certainly.
( )	3. Why must use the special polish rag to dry the car?	C. He wants to have a five-thousand-kilometer basic maintenance.
( )	4. What do the repairmen need to pay special attention to when waxing?	D. Because a common rag has fluff which will stick to its surface.
( )	5. Do we need to wait until the wax is dry before we rub it clean?	E. Make sure no dust is on the surface.

Part Four：Practice

Ⅰ. Complete these sentences with the words and phrases in the box.

> at low speed, up and down, flush away, generally speaking, comes to an end, divided into, backward and forward, charge for, according to, dry, basic maintenance, rub

1. We have to _____ the parts.
2. Your warranty _____.
3. I drive my car _____.
4. Body waxes are _____ two kinds.
5. You just use them _____ the directions.
6. _____ the dust and the sand on the surface of the car with water.
7. _____, hard wax lasts longer.

8. Wash it _____ at first, and then _____.
9. Do I need to wait until the wax is _____ before I _____ it clean.
10. I'd like to have a five-thousand-kilometer _____.

Ⅱ. Match the following Chinese with English expressions.

( )	1. repairs	A. 打蜡
( )	2. basic maintenance	B. 维修单
( )	3. wax	C. 修理费
( )	4. warranty certificate	D. 基础护理
( )	5. maintaining sheet	E. 保修卡

Ⅲ. Put the following sentences into English.

1. 没什么大问题，我马上就能修好。(Nothing serious, I...)
2. 您要洗车打蜡吗？(Would you like to...)
3. 我想做一个基础维护。(I'd like to...)
4. 我们要收取零件费。(Charge for)
5. 您的保修单过期了。(come to an end)

Ⅳ. Complete the following tasks.

1. Play the parts in the dialogues.
2. Make a dialogue according to the following situation: A customer wants to ask for a five-thousand-kilometer basic maintenance.

Ⅴ. Self-check.

I learned:

( ) communicate   ( ) maintain   ( ) warranty   ( ) describe
( ) basic   ( ) wax   ( ) surface   ( ) scratch
( ) sponge   ( ) beautify   ( ) direction

I can:

( ) collect useful information of maintenance.
( ) give some maintenace suggestions.

 Lesson 12

Motor Insurance

Learning Objectives

Master the basic knowledge and skills	
➤ Language learning objective	Grasp the new words and useful expressions.
➤ Skill learning objective	Be able to know the risks of insurance and the insurance premium of different vehicles.
Develop core competences of English	
➤ Know the culture and emotions conveyed by different texts on "Motor Insurance" topic. ➤ Know the differences between Chinese and Western thinking in English expression. ➤ Develop the pragmatic competence in motor insurance scene.	

Part One: Warming-up

 Make your choice:

1. If you are a customer, when you walk into an insurance company, you hope you will:
   ( ) Receive a warm reception.
   ( ) Get professional services.
   ( ) Not waste any time there.

 What else?

2. If you are an **insurance agent**, how should you **receive** your costumers?
   ( ) Introduce and give customers my name cards.
   ( ) Explain their questions clearly.
   ( ) Keep a smile all the way.

What else?

insurance agent 保险代理
receive 接待

Module Two Business English 商务英语

 As an agent, you should:

1. Tell the differences among different car risks clearly.
2. Guide your customers to choose a suitable car risk.

Part Two: New Words and Useful Expressions

Ⅰ. New words.

serve	*v.* 服务，招待
suit	*v.* 适合
insure	*n.* 保险 *v.* 投保
premium	*n.* 保险费
Insurance Company	*n.* 保险公司
agent	*n.* 代理人
risk	*n.* 险别
risks covered	*n.* 保险范围
recommend	*v.* 推荐
calculate	*v.* 计算
third person liability	*n.* 第三者责任险
insurance policy	*n.* 保险单
all risk	*n.* 全险

Ⅱ. Useful expressions.

1. I am looking for insurances from your company.
2. Please fill in the application form.
3. What risks should be covered?
4. Let's leave insurance now.
5. It's better for you to see the leaflet, and then make a decision.
6. The total premium is 2,100 Yuan.
7. What's the insurance premium?
8. These kinds of risks suit your car.
9. Do you want car insurance?
10. I would like to get insurance for my car, may I talk to an agent, please?

1. 我是来贵公司投保的。
2. 请填写一下保单。
3. 您看应该保哪些险？
4. 好吧，保险的问题就谈到这里。
5. 您最好先看看说明书，再决定保什么险。
6. 保险费总共是2100元。
7. 保险费是多少？
8. 这些险种适合您的车。
9. 您想要给车买保险吗？
10. 我想为我的车买保险，我能和代理谈一下吗？

Part Three: Situations

Situation A

Do you want insurance?

> Dick wants to buy insurance for his car, and he asks John something about insurance…

(D—Dick, J—John, R—Receptionist, B—Bob)

D: Hi! John, I need to get car insurance, do you have any ideas?

J: Well, you can **consult** The People's Insurance Company of China.

D: Do they insure cars?

J: As far as I know, they insure all kinds of **vehicles**.

D: And are their rates low?

J: Not low, but reasonable, I've always got good service from them.

D: What risks does The People's Insurance Company of China cover?

J: I'm not clear. Let me give you their phone number and you can call them.

D: Thank you, I'll call them later.

(Ring, Ring…)

R: Hello, Good afternoon, The People's Insurance Company of China. How may I help you?

D: Good afternoon, I would like to get insurance for my car. May I talk to an agent, please?

R: Please **hold the line**. I'll transfer you to an agent.

B: Hello, this is Bob speaking. How may I help you?

D: Yes, I'd like to get insurance for my car.

B: OK. What kind of car do you have?

D: It is a Aeolus S30. I bought it last year.

B: What kind of **deductible** would you like to have? Our regular policy is 25% deductible.

D: What does it mean?

B: A deductible is the amount the insurance would not pay. For example, if the repair charge is 1,000 Yuan and deductible is 25%, the Insurance Company would only pay 750 Yuan.

D: Oh, I see.

B: We recommend a third person liability, and property damage liability.

D: How much would that cost me?

consult 参考，查阅，咨询

vehicle 车辆，运载工具

hold the line 请稍等

deductible（尤指税收、应纳税的收入中）可扣除的，本课为免赔率

B: Give me a few minutes to calculate the premium.

D: OK.

B: The premium is 1,250 Yuan before **sales tax**.

D: That's a little expensive.

B: Our rates are very **competitive**.

D: OK, I will think it over.

B: Of course. If you are free, you'd better come to our company. I'll show you an insurance rate and its detailed information.

D: I'll take your advice.

B: You can also call me if you want to know more information about the car insurance. My telephone number is 87294538.

D: That's very kind of you.

B: It's my pleasure. Any more questions?

D: No, thanks.

B: OK, have a good day.

D: The same to you. Bye.

B: Bye.

sales tax 营业税

competitive
有竞争力的（价格）

Notes

1. The People's Insurance Company of China 中国人民保险公司
2. How may I help you 等同于 Can I help you 但是前者显得更加有礼貌
3. third person liability 意为"第三者责任险"，property damage liability 意为"财产损失险"
4. Our rates are very competitive. competitive 是"很有竞争性"的意思，在这里此句话可以意为"我们的费率已经很低了"

 Make your choice according to situation A.

	Questions	Answers
( )	1. What is Bob?	A. His number is 87294538.
( )	2. What kind is Dick's car?	B. It is a Aeolus S30, he bought it last year.
( )	3. Is John an agent?	C. A deductible is the amount the insurance would not pay.
( )	4. What does deductible mean?	D. No, he is Dick's friend.
( )	5. What's Bob's phone number?	E. He is an insurance agent.

Situation B

I want to know something about car insurance.

> Mr. William wants to buy insurance for his car. Mr. Zhang meets him in the office of The People's Insurance Company of China.

(W—Mr. William, Z—Mr. Zhang)

W: Is there anybody in?

Z: Yes, what can I do for you, sir?

W: I am **looking for** insurance in your company, I want to know something about car insurance.

Z: It's my pleasure, please.

W: Recently, I've bought a new car. Unluckly, I had an accident 5 days ago. So, I want to buy insurance for it.

Z: Oh, I see.

W: What risks should I buy?

Z: Is it a **private** car?

W: Yes, for private cars, what kind of risk can your company provide for me?

Z: Do you mind I ask you several questions?

W: Never mind, please.

Z: How old are you, and what do you do for a living?

W: I'm 35 years old and I'm a teacher.

Z: Do you often drive your car?

W: Sometimes.

Z: According to your case, we recommend you to buy "Economy insurance" plan——compulsory traffic insurance+vehicle damage+third person liability+deductible-free risk. I think these risks suit your car.

W: En, what's the insurance premium?

Z: Give me a few minutes. Let me calculate the premium.

W: OK.

Z: The total premium is 2,100 Yuan **annually**.

W: Your price seems a little high.

Z: We could make them lower for you. For detailed directions, you can read an insurance policy.

W: Can you give me one? I'll discuss them with my family.

Z: Of course. I'll give you at once.

W: Thank you.

look for 寻找

private 私有的

annually 每年

Z: Here you are.

W: Thank you. And I'd like to take these **catalogs**.

Z: Sure, please.

W: And I also want these price lists.

Z: Please take them as you like. Here's my **name card**. If you are not clear, call me please.

W: OK. Thank you.

Z: By the way, could I have a calling card of yours?

W: Yes, here it is.

Z: Thanks.

W: I hope I can do business with you. See you later.

Z: See you.

catalog 目录，商品目录

name card 名片

 Notes

1. Economy insurance 经济保险方案。险种组合：交强险+车辆损失险+第三者责任险+不计免赔特约险。
2. a calling card = a name card 名片

 Make your choice according to situation B.

	Questions	Answers
( )	1. Where does Mr. William meet Mr. Zhang?	A. Yes, he does.
( )	2. Why does Mr. William want to buy insurance for his car?	B. He is a teacher.
( )	3. What does Mr. William do for a living?	C. It is 2,100 Yuan annually.
( )	4. What's the insurance premium of "Economy insurance"?	D. They meet in the office of The People's Insurance Company of China.
( )	5. Does Mr. Zhang give Mr. William his name card?	E. He had an accident 5 days ago.

Part Four: Practice

Ⅰ. Complete these sentences with the words and phrases in the box.

> service, name, looking for, transfer, provide, pay, cover, a living, risk, whatever

1. I'm _____ insurance from your company.
2. What kind of _____ should I buy?
3. Can you _____ price lists for me?
4. Are you planning to _____ in cash?
5. Do you have a _____ card?
6. I'll _____ you to an agent.
7. What risk does your company be able to _____?
8. What do you do for _____?
9. I've always got good _____ from them.
10. Please take _____ you like.

Ⅱ. Match the following Chinese with English expressions.

( )	全险	A. all risk
( )	保险公司	B. catalog
( )	保险代理人	C. a calling card
( )	价目单	D. insurance agent
( )	名片	E. insurance company

Ⅲ. Translate the following sentences into English.

1. 我想为我的车买份保险。(I want to...)
2. 保险费一年是多少？(What's the insurance... annually?)
3. 一般来说，汽车有哪些险种？(Generally speaking...?)
4. 您能给我一份保险的资料吗？(Can you give...?)
5. 我想要这些价目表。(I would like to take...)
6. 我希望能和你合作。(I hope...)

Ⅳ. Complete the following tasks.

1. Play the parts in the dialogues.
2. Make a dialogue according to the next situation: Supposing you are a insurance agent, a taxi driver asks you something about car insurance.

Ⅴ. Self-check.

I learned:

( ) risk　　( ) insurance　　( ) agent　　( ) serve
( ) suit　　( ) calculate　　( ) policy　　( ) liability
( ) deductible　　( ) tax　　( ) competitive　　( ) private

I can:

( ) tell the risks of insurance to customer.
( ) talk about the insurance premium.

附 录

附录A 汽车标志

Logo	Brand	Notes
	Mercedes-Benz 梅赛德斯奔驰	Representing the dominance over land, sea and air. 代表奔驰汽车统领海陆空
	BMW 宝马	The white against the blue represents white clouds, blue sky and rotating propeller. 蓝天映衬着白色代表了蓝天、白云和旋转不停的螺旋桨
	Audi 奥迪	The four rings represent the four companies of the Auto-Union consortium of 1932. It's the symbol of unity. 四环代表着1932年成立的汽车联盟的四家分公司，是团结的象征
	Volkswagen 大众	The logo contains the letters V and W: V means people and W means car, which indicates the car is designed for the common people. 标志包含字母V和W：字母V代表人民，W代表汽车，寓意是为普通人而设计的车
	Opel 欧宝	The shape of the lightning represents speed and outstanding. 闪电形状代表速度和卓越
	Skoda 斯柯达	A flying arrow with the bird wing: Bird wing is the symbol of technological progress and worldwide product marketing, the arrow is the symbol of advanced technology. 飞翔之箭：鸟翼象征着技术进步和产品行销全世界；飞行的箭象征先进的工艺
	Aston Martin 阿斯顿·马丁	The flying wings represents sprint speed and lofty ideals. 展翅飞翔的大鹏，有着从天而降的冲刺速度和远大的理想
	Bentley 宾利	A pair of eagle wings. 一对雄鹰的翅膀
	ROLLS-ROYCE 劳斯莱斯	Two Rs represent harmonious relationship. 两个"R"代表和睦的关系，你中有我，我中有你

（续）

Logo	Brand	Notes
	Toyota 丰田	Three ellipses indicate the company is customer-oriented, product-oriented and technology-oriented. 三个椭圆表示丰田公司是以顾客为导向，以产品为导向和以技术为导向的
	Lexus 雷克萨斯	Taking the first letter of Lexus, it represents 'luxury' and 'elegance'. 取"Lexus"的首字母 L，代表豪华和高雅
	Mazda 马自达	"V" represents outstretched wings of seagull. It flies all over the world. V 代表海鸥伸展的翅膀，它能飞向全世界
	Peugeot 标致	A mighty lion represents the statue of liberty. 雄狮代表着自由
	Citroen 雪铁龙	Use the shape of the gear as trademarks. The founder invented the herringbone gear. 利用齿轮的形状作为商标，其创始人发明了人字齿轮
	Lamborghini 兰博基尼	A bullheaded cattle reflects the product features, which are high-power, high-speed sports car. 一头公牛，体现其产品的特点：大功率和高速
	Ferrari 法拉利	A leaping horse brings you good luck. 一匹跃起的马，可以带来好运
	Jaguar 捷豹	The leaping jaguar represents the power, speed, and quickness of its cars. 前扑的美洲豹子，代表车的动力、速度及反应灵敏
	Ford 福特	The logo looks like a little rabbit, for Henry Ford likes small animals. 看上去像一只奔跑的小兔子，因为福特喜欢小动物
	HYUNDAI 现代	The ellipse represents the earth or steering-wheel. H is the first letter of Hyundai. 椭圆代表地球或转向盘，H 是 Hyundai 的首字母

附　录

（续）

Logo	Brand	Notes
	Hongqi 红旗	Symbolizing nobleness and gorgeousness. 象征高贵、华丽
	BYD 比亚迪	Build you dream. 成就梦想
	Chery 奇瑞	Letter A shapes like human body, which represents people-oriented awareness. A 形状像人体，代表公司以人为本的经营理念
	Dong feng 东风	Two swallows are dancing against the wind. 双燕舞东风
	Tesla 特斯拉	Go Electric. 电动出行
	Geely 吉利	Happy life, Geely drive. 快乐生活，吉利驾驶
	NIO 蔚来	A New Day, Which meansblue sky coming. 新的一天，蓝天再现
	BAIC 北京	It symbolizes Beijing, China and it is like a cheering human figure. "北"既象征了中国北京，又好似一个欢呼雀跃的人形
	DENZA 腾势	On a quest for progress, 追求美好。Rising momentum, electric future. 腾势而起，电动未来

附录 B 参 考 译 文

模块一：汽车英语

第 1 课
汽 车 类 型

世界上有各种类型的汽车，可以分为三大类。每种类型包括不同种类的汽车，概括如下。

1. 旅行车和越野车

旅行车以消遣娱乐为目的，可长距离旅行；而越野车如吉普车、运动型多功能车可以在条件恶劣的路面上行驶。

2. 轿车和轻型商用车

轿车是一种家庭日常用车，可以容纳 4~6 人。这种车还包括轻型商用车，如轻型货车，用于轻型负载。

3. 重型汽车

货车属于这类汽车，用来装载一些重的货物，铰接车和自卸车也属于这一类型。公共汽车是另一种重型车，根据其长度和设计，公共汽车分为小型、中型、大型和铰接型。农用车也属于重型汽车，如拖拉机。

此外还有许多特殊用途的汽车也属于重型汽车，如洒水车、救护车、消防车等。这些汽车在我们的日常生活中为我们服务。

第 2 课
汽车发动机 1

发动机给汽车提供动力，它能把燃料变成汽车的能量。如果没有发动机，汽车将不能移动，所以发动机通常被称为汽车的心脏。发动机可按照以下方式进行分类。

1. 燃料类型：汽油发动机、柴油发动机、燃气发动机。
2. 气缸的数量：2 缸至 12 缸。
3. 气缸的排列：直列式（3~5 缸）、V 形（6 缸、8 缸、10 缸、12 缸）、水平对置式。
4. 容量或排量：1.5~5L。
5. 配气机构：底置式凸轮轴、顶置凸轮轴、单顶置凸轮轴和双顶置凸轮轴。配气机构由进、排气门、凸轮轴、气门油封、气门弹簧、气门挺杆组成。
6. 每一次循环冲程数：二冲程、四冲程。
7. 点火方式：点燃式、压燃式。
8. 冷却方式：风冷式、水冷式。

9. 涡轮增压：有些发动机带有涡轮增压器，它能使更多的空气进入气缸，这就大大增强了发动机的性能。

第 3 课
汽车发动机 2

1. 燃油供给系统：发动机的燃油供给系统可以把汽油从燃油箱里抽出来并使它与空气混合，这样适当浓度的空气和汽油的混合物就能进入气缸。

2. 润滑系统：润滑系统要确保发动机中的每一个活动部件都能获得机油以使其能顺畅地运转。需要机油的两大主要部件是活塞和轴承，它们能让曲轴和凸轮轴这类部件自如旋转。

3. 冷却系统：大多数汽车上的冷却系统是由散热器和水泵组成的。冷却液在气缸周围循环流动，经散热器冷却。

4. 点火系统：点火系统产生高压电，并将其传输到火花塞，点燃气缸中的空气燃料混合气，这就开始了做功行程。

5. 起动系统：起动机是电动机，它能让发动机起动。

第 4 课
汽车底盘 1

底盘是汽车的底部部件。它由传动系统、行驶系统、转向系统和制动系统组成。底盘有三个主要功能：1）支撑和安置车身、发动机以及汽车其他主要部件；2）接收和传递发动机的动力；3）确保车辆的正常行驶。底盘的主要部件有：悬架、车架、弹簧、减振器、传动轴、制动器、轮胎和车轮。

悬架有两大主要部件。

1. 前悬架

前悬架可以允许前轮上下移动，并可以吸收路面振动。还可以允许前轮左右摆动，以便使汽车转动。

2. 后悬架

后悬架使用钢板弹簧，安装在一个车轮上。钢板弹簧固定在三个点上，即前支架、后吊耳和桥壳。

第 5 课
汽车底盘四大系统

1. 传动系统

传动系统能把发动机的动力传递到驱动轮，并能保证车辆在各种条件下正常行驶。其主要部件有：离合器、变速器、传动轴、主减速器、差速器、万向节、半轴和传动轴。

2. 行驶系统

行驶系统有三个基本功能：接收传动轴的动力，支撑汽车的总重量，缓和不平路面对车身造成的冲击，从而给乘客提供舒适的乘车体验。行驶系统的主要部件有：车架、车桥、悬架、车轮和轮胎。

3. 转向系统

转向系统是一种转向操纵机构和转向传动机构。主要部件有：转向盘、转向器、转向轴、转向减振器、横拉杆和转向臂。

4. 制动系统

制动系统的主要作用是使行驶中的汽车按照驾驶人的要求进行减速或者停车，其主要部件有：制动踏板、制动盘、制动鼓、制动总泵和制动阀。

第 6 课
电气系统的组成

电气系统是汽车的重要组成部分，其性能好坏影响汽车的动力性、经济性、可靠性、安全性、舒适性等，其科技含量已成为衡量现代汽车档次的重要标志之一。现代汽车所装备的电气系统，按其用途可划分为以下四个部分。

1. 充电系统包括蓄电池、发电机及电压调节器。它是用来给蓄电池充电的，并为电子元件和其他电子系统提供电能。

2. 用电系统包括起动系统、点火系统、仪表系统、照明与信号系统、电子控制系统以及辅助电器。

3. 检测系统包括各种检测仪表和各种报警灯，用来检测发动机和其他装置的工作情况。

4. 配电系统包括中央接线盒、电路开关、保险装置、导线等，以保证线路工作的可靠性和安全性。

另外，电动汽车还包括动力电池管理系统、电机驱动系统、整车控制系统代替发动机和变速器。

第 7 课
电气系统分类

电力系统是电气系统中非常重要的部分。它主要包含点火系统，起动系统和仪表系统等。

所有汽油发动机都需要某种形式的点火系统。该系统由蓄电池，点火开关，分电器，点火线圈，火花塞，电阻，低压和高压电线组成。

它具有两个功能：一个是从电池低电压升压到高电压，另一个是控制点火定时以满足发动机的需要。它还具有两个电路：一次电路和二次电路。

起动系统是电气系统的心脏。它提供了起动发动机的动力。它由电池、起动开关、起动继电器、起动电动机组成。

此外，还有其他系统。它们是照明系统，喇叭系统和空调系统。它们与电气系统关系密切。

第 8 课
汽 车 车 身

车身是驾驶人工作、乘载乘客和货物的地方。它包括车篷、车门、后挡板、后视镜、挡泥板、栅格、前照灯和尾灯。车身起保护发动机、乘客和货物的作用。

目前，车身形状主要有七类。
1. 轿车车身：有前后两排座椅，可以容纳 4~6 人，可分为两门或四门轿车。
2. 敞篷车车身：这种车的顶部用乙烯树脂制成，可升可降。
3. 两厢两门或掀背式车身：这种车的显著特征是有后行李舱，这样乘客可拥有更大的空间。
4. 旅行车车身：旅行车最大特点是它的顶部。它的车顶延伸了平直的背部，并且在车的后部有一个宽敞的行李舱。
5. 轻型货车车身：这种车的设计使驾驶室的后面可直接装载货物。
6. 搬运车车身：这种车的顶部很高，可装载大型货物，并拥有足够的空间。
7. 运动型多功能车车身：这种车的设计多种多样。

第 9 课
燃油经济性

汽车的燃油经济性是指使用单位体积燃油的行驶距离。它可以用每升公里（km/L）或每加仑英里（MPG）来测量。油耗是衡量汽车燃油经济性的重要指标。它是每单位距离消耗的燃料量，例如，每 100 公里的公升（L/100km）。它包括等速油耗和循环油耗。

等速油耗：等速油耗是指汽车在良好路面上等速行驶时的燃油经济性指标。不过，由于汽车在实际行驶中经常出现加速、减速、制动和发动机怠速等多种工作情况，因此等速油耗往往偏低，与实际油耗有较大差别。

道路循环油耗：是汽车在道路上按照规定的车速和时间规范作反复循环行驶时所测定的燃油经济性指标，也叫作多工况道路循环油耗。

第 10 课
汽车安全设备、舒适设备和操控性

汽车安全是车辆不可或缺的部分。它可以分为主动安全和被动安全。主动安全配置就是预防车辆发生事故的安全配置。例如常见的 ABS、EBD、ESP 等。所以，主动安全配置更加重要一些。被动安全配置就是在事故发生后，避免车内人员少受伤害的安全配置，例如常见的气囊等。

舒适性的指标包括车内噪声，车内空间大小，悬架的过滤性，座椅的支撑性、材质和功能，变速器的舒适性和平顺性等。

车辆操控性的好坏主要由动力、悬架和转向系统三个因素来决定。动力是操控性的根本，悬架是操控性的关键，转向系统是操控性的保障。

第 11 课
新能源汽车

新能源汽车是指除汽油、柴油发动机之外所有其他能源汽车，包括燃料电池汽车、混合动力汽车、氢能源动力汽车和太阳能汽车等。

电动汽车的组成包括电力驱动及控制系统、驱动力传动等机械系统、完成既定任务的工作装置等。电力驱动及控制系统是电动汽车的核心,由驱动电机、电源和电机调速控制装置等组成。

纯电动汽车应用前景广泛,具有无污染、低噪声、高能效等优点。但蓄电池单位重量储存的能量太小,充电后持续行驶里程不理想。

模块二:商务英语

第1课 客户开发

A 我要……接电话。

(刘小姐正在打电话,她想告诉布朗先生来提车,但是她把电话打到史密斯太太家了。)
(刘——刘小姐,简——史密斯太太,史——史密斯先生)

刘:你好,我是吉亨汽车销售公司的刘艳,您是布朗先生吗?您订购的车已经到了。
简:恐怕您打错了电话,我们没有订车。
刘:真的吗?
简:是的,我丈夫没有跟我讲过这件事。
刘:等一等,这是布朗先生家的电话吗?
简:不,这是史密斯家。
刘:对不起,打扰您了。
简:没关系。
刘:史密斯太太,目前我们店有款新能源电动车做活动,性价比非常高,您感兴趣吗?
简:嗯,这个嘛,我得和我丈夫商量。
刘:哦,知道了。什么时候可以给您丈夫打电话?
简:他通常六点到家。
刘:我知道了。等一会我再打电话过来,我想不会打扰你们吃晚饭。
简:我们晚饭时间通常在六点半左右。
刘:谢谢,我待会儿再打过来。

(六点钟后,刘小姐又打电话到史密斯家)

刘:喂,您是史密斯先生吗?今天下午我打电话给您太太,她要我这个时候打电话给您。请问您打算购买新能源电动汽车吗?
史:嗯,你能介绍下吗?
刘:我们店有款电动车性价比非常高,您什么时候有空到4S店来,我跟您详细介绍。
史:下周末有空。
刘:我知道了,届时我会跟您联络,再见。

B 您是明天上午还是下午有时间?

(刘艳正在打电话,跟亨特先生预约。)
(刘——刘小姐 亨——亨特)

刘：请问是亨特先生吗？

亨：我就是。

刘：亨特先生，我是吉亨汽车销售公司的刘艳。昨天您来我们店咨询，对我们的车表现了极大的兴趣，但是很快离开了，所以我没能向您介绍我们的服务。

亨：我当时有个电话，不得不离开。请继续说。

刘：亨特先生，您对我们店的哪款车感兴趣，是燃油车还是电动车？

亨：我想买燃油车，我对风神 AX7 这款车感兴趣。

刘：您真有眼力，我们肯定能满足您的需求。我能提个建议吗？

亨：当然可以。

刘：假如您方便的话，您明天可以来我们店，我将向您做详细的说明。这样您就可以更清楚地了解这款车。

亨：行，大概需要多长时间？

刘：不超过一个小时。您明天上午或是下午有空吗？

亨：最好是明天下午。

刘：下午两点半钟，行吗？

亨：行。

刘：好的，明天下午我会在店里等您，明天见！

亨：明天见！

第 2 课　客 户 接 待

A 我喜欢自驾游。

（格雷先生来到一个 4S 店，刘小姐——这家车店的销售员，接待了他。）

（刘——刘小姐，格——格雷先生）

刘：早上好，欢迎光临本店！

格：早上好。

刘：我叫刘艳，是本店的销售员，请问您贵姓？

格：我叫杰弗里·格雷。我周末喜欢自驾游，想买款节油的车，能推荐适合我的车吗？

刘：非常乐意。风神 E70 是我们店里的畅销车型。这款车是新能源电动车，节能、环保，电池续航是 500km，并且 10 年质保，不限里程。这款车非常适合您周末自驾游。

格：听起来不错。还有其他款式的电动汽车吗？

刘：还有一款风神奕炫 EV，这款车外观非常时尚，内饰舒适，适合您这样时髦的人。感兴趣的话，您可以坐进车里体验下。我敢打赌您一定会喜欢它的。

格：真的吗？我得仔细瞧瞧。

B 您在哪里工作？

（布莱克先生，一位工人，来到了一家 4S 店，刘小姐接待了他。）

（刘——刘小姐，布——布莱克先生）

刘：先生，下午好。欢迎光临本店！

布：下午好！
刘：我叫刘艳，本店的销售员。希望您能喜欢我的服务，我能认识您一下吗？
布：我叫吉姆·布莱克。
刘：很高兴见到您，布莱克先生。你看起来像一位教师，是吗？
布：不，我不是。实际上，我是个工人。我在一家钢铁厂工作。
刘：您来过我们 4S 店看过车吗？
布：没有，但是我已经去过几家 4S 店了。
刘：您考虑什么类型的车呢？
布：我喜欢 SUV，后备厢容量要大。
刘：嗯，您来本店算是来对了。瞧，难道那辆多功能车不适合您吗？
布：这款车，我知道，我在网上搜索过关于这款车的资料。
刘：我相信您对这款车的情况应该有了一定的了解，但是 80% 的性能需要试驾才能体验出来，如果您的时间允许，我可以安排您试驾。
布：那再好不过了。
刘：请问，您带了驾照了吗？
布：带了。
刘：好的，请您到这边来办理试驾手续。

第 3 课　信 息 收 集

A　您喜欢新能源车吗？

（多得先生走进了一家 4S 店，刘艳接待了他并问了他几个问题。）

（刘——刘小姐，多——多得先生）

刘：先生，您需要帮忙吗？
多：是的，但是我需要先看一看车。
刘：您将什么时候用车？
多：元旦之前。我认为元旦是一个新的开始。
刘：好主意！主要是谁用车呢？
多：我妻子。
刘：我猜您妻子是事业有成的人，对不对？
多：她是位销售人员。您知道，作为一名销售人员，她每天要跑很多的路。
刘：她喜欢新能源车吗？
多：当然。
刘：是的，电动车低噪声，高能效，非常适合你妻子用。她喜欢什么颜色？
多：喜欢白色。
刘：她喜欢轿车还是运动型多用途车？
多：轿车。
刘：她喜不喜欢混合动力汽车？
多：不，她喜欢纯电动车。

刘：那就对了，现在是购买纯电动车非常好的时机，技术成熟，充电桩普及，并且还有免购置税的优惠政策。瞧那辆车，我们正好有辆车，能满足您的需求。

B 您的车况很差了。

（刘艳正在和柯林斯先生交谈以获得更多的信息。）
（刘——刘小姐 柯——柯林斯先生）

刘：您好，我是刘艳，您贵姓？
柯：你好，我是吉姆·柯林斯。
刘：我问您几个问题您不会介意吧？
柯：不会，请讲。
刘：您家有几口人？
柯：4口人，我有两个孩子。
刘：哦，我想您一定是个好父亲，平时经常陪伴孩子吧？
柯：我是个律师，平时很忙。但是周末我会开车带家人们到郊外游玩。
刘：您现在的车跑得怎么样？
柯：不是很好，我的车已经用了8年了。
刘：目前您的车主要问题是什么？
柯：我的车很旧了，而且总需要修理。我的车没有导航系统，出去自驾游非常不方便。
刘：确实，现在很多车都自带"智能车机系统"，为驾车带来了便利和娱乐性。那发动机呢？
柯：发动机的驱动力不强劲并且起动不够快。
刘：哦，您的车况现在已经很差了。您考虑现在换新车吗？
柯：当然，越快越好！

第 4 课　汽车介绍

A 您对哪款车感兴趣？

（鲁先生正在给福特先生介绍汽车。）
（鲁——鲁先生，福——福特先生）

鲁：福特先生，您对哪款车感兴趣？
福：我对风神 AX7 感兴趣，你能跟我介绍这款车吗？
鲁：当然可以。首先它是一款5座位的 SUV，长度是 4645mm，轴距是 2715mm，乘坐空间十分宽敞。这款车的中控屏幕是 10.25 英寸触摸屏，可实现智能双屏互动，带有"智能车机系统"。
福：对不起，打断一下，你能详细说下"智能车机系统"吗？我很感兴趣。
鲁：行，当然可以。"智能车机系统"拥有 ETC 通行、5G 无线通信、GPS 导航、出行导游、购物、娱乐影音等多种功能的车载终端。这款 AX7 配的是 WindLink3.0 人工智能车机系统，具备硬件配置高、极简 UI 体验、极速 AI 语音等亮点。通过语音就可以控制，在开车途中使用起来更加安全便捷。同时 WindLink3.0 还可以与手机等智能产品自动产生

互联，带来更多的娱乐性。
福：听起来，非常有趣。我已经迫不及待想体验这个系统了。
鲁：当然可以，您请上车亲自体验。

B 我能问您一些问题吗？

（琼斯先生打算买一辆车，他正在问鲁志一些问题。）
（鲁——鲁先生，琼——琼斯先生）

琼：鲁先生，我能问您一些问题吗？
鲁：可以，请问。
琼：这辆车的油耗如何？
鲁：手动档每100公里油耗7升，自动档每100公里油耗7.2升。
琼：该车的最大速度是多少？
鲁：手动档195km/h，自动档180km/h。
琼：该车是前轮驱动、后轮驱动还是四轮驱动？
鲁：是后轮驱动。
琼：发动机有4个气缸还是6个气缸？
鲁：4个气缸。
琼：发动机是直列式、V形排列还是水平对置排列？
鲁：是直列式。
琼：气缸排量是多少？
鲁：是1.6升。
琼：车的变速器呢？
鲁：它有5个手动档和4个自动档。
琼：这辆车有什么安全设备？
鲁：它有驾驶人和前排乘客安全气囊、侧安全气囊、安全带、防抱死制动系统、电子制动装置和驱动防滑系统等。
琼：好，就到这里。非常感谢您的帮助。
鲁：不客气。

第5课 价格协商

A 请问这个车多少钱？

（马克斯先生来到4S店。鲁志正在向马克斯先生介绍车辆的情况，但是马克斯先生几次打断鲁志的讲话。）
（鲁——鲁先生，马——马克斯先生）

鲁：现在让我们来谈一谈发动机。
马：打扰一下，请问这车多少钱？
鲁：（不理睬马克斯）气缸排量是1.6升。
马：请问这车多少钱？

鲁：请等一下，我很快就会讲到价格。现在让我们来讲讲车的经济性。

马：这车到底是多少钱？

鲁：我很快就会谈到车价，但是这不是最重要的事情。我只是想让您对车有更多的了解，而且您肯定会发现这是一笔合算的交易。所以请别着急，先听我说好吗？

马：好吧。

鲁：最后，车的最大速度是手动档195km/h，自动档180km/h。好了，我知道您现在开始喜欢这款车了，并且我相信当您发现这是一笔很合算的交易时，您一定会激动不已。

马：真的吗？

鲁：好吧，车的价格是￥132,000。

B 价格不能再低些吗？

（马克斯先生正在和鲁先生协商价格。）
（鲁——鲁先生，马——马克斯先生）

鲁：您已经决定买那款车了吗？

马：是的。

鲁：好的，马克斯先生，请到我的办公室来。

马：行。这款车有促销和折扣吗？

鲁：很抱歉地告诉您，我们不打折并且促销活动昨天已经结束了。

马：难道就不能延迟一天吗？

鲁：不能。您知道，作为一个知名的公司，我们必须守信用，抱歉。

马：没什么。

鲁：那么您的预算是多少呢？

马：那你们车价是多少呢？

鲁：￥132,000。

马：但我的预算是13万。

鲁：坦率地说，我们不能接受您的价位。如果按照您的开价，恐怕一些配置就没有了。￥131,500怎么样？

马：还是超过了我的预算。能否再低一些？

鲁：行，￥131,000怎么样？我只能出这个价了。

马：好吧，成交！

鲁：谢谢。你是用现金还是信用卡付费？

马：用信用卡。

鲁：谢谢！

第6课 车辆交付

A 您什么时候来提车？

（鲁先生正在打电话，确认提车时间。）
（鲁——鲁先生，王——王先生）

鲁：您好，我是鲁志，可以请王先生接电话吗？

王：您好，请问您是谁？

鲁：早晨好，王先生。我是奥迪4S店的推销员。您上周购买的新车已经到店。您能告诉我什么时候可以取货吗？

王：我星期天有空。

鲁：好。我们需要在交货前进行出厂前检查。此外，我们将会彻底清洗新车。那么，星期天上午11：00怎么样。

王：可以。

鲁：您需要我们提供接送服务吗？

王：不用了，谢谢。我可以乘出租车去那里。我需要准备什么？

鲁：请提前准备身份证，合同和尾款。

王：我应该为交货过程留出多少时间？

鲁：整个交付过程主要包括车辆检查和操作，支付尾款，文件填写和交付仪式。至少需要3个小时。请给自己尽可能多的时间。

王：好的。星期天上午11：00见。

鲁：我期待与您见面！再见。

B 车辆验收需要注意什么？

（王先生来到4S店提车。）

（鲁——鲁先生，王——王先生）

鲁：早上好，王先生！欢迎来店提车。

王：早上好，请您介绍一下提车过程？

鲁：今天，我们将在您提车之前对它进行检查。

王：验车要注意什么？

鲁：这是一份在接受之前要注意的事项清单。您应注意以下部分：车辆外部，内部，配件等。您要首先检查哪一部分？

王：让我们检查一下车的外观。

鲁：请绕着汽车走，检查是否有在运输过程中可能会产生的凹痕或划痕。

王：油漆、装饰或玻璃上没有缺陷。

鲁：请检查所有配件是否工作正常，诸如蓝牙连接，车载收音机，指示器，风窗玻璃刮水器等。

王：我确定我签约的合同中所有的功能和附件都已安装。那下一部分呢？

鲁：您应该确保所有安全功能都放心使用，例如后视摄像头，后备传感器或胎压监测系统。

王：好的，让我调整一下这些设备。

鲁：新车将在油箱中注满1/4的燃油。

王：是的，仍然有1/4的汽油。

鲁：现在您已经对汽车进行了彻底检查。如果没有损坏，请在这些文件上签名。

王：是的，一切都很好。我在上面签名。

附 录

第7课 支付方式

A 我要分期付款。

（怀特刚刚和鲁志谈论签订合同，他决定买下这辆车）

（鲁——鲁先生，怀——怀特先生）

鲁：我很高兴我们的交易进展顺利。

怀：我也一样。我非常喜爱这款车——12万元，白色风神AX7。

鲁：您刚刚做了一个明智的决定。

怀：现在我想讨论一下支付方式。我能通过银行汇款付款吗？

鲁：对不起，恐怕不行。我们只接受现金和信用卡付款。

怀：噢，我现在没有足够的现金，而且也没有信用卡。

鲁：那我们的分期付款方式能解决问题。

怀：我不太清楚分期付款。你能做个简短的说明吗？

鲁：当然。如果您选择分期付款，您应该在汽车运送前一周支付首期款，首期款也叫定金，然后在运送前一天支付中期款，最后在收到汽车后付清余款。

怀：听起来很合理，但是我首期付款要多少？

鲁：4万元，总价的1/3。

怀：太好了，我现在就付款。

鲁：好的，这边请。

B 您知道我们的支付方式吗？

（鲁志刚刚和格林太太进行了一场愉快的交谈，格林太太已经决定向他购买汽车。）

（鲁——鲁先生，格——格林太太）

鲁：很高兴能与像您这样的女士合作。

格：我想向您买车也是一种缘分。

鲁：是啊，太好了。您知道我们的付款方式吗？

格：不知道，是什么呢？

鲁：我们既接受现金也接受信用卡。另外，您也可以采用分期付款方式。

格：信用卡支付和分期付款之间有什么不同吗？

鲁：是的，如果您用信用卡或者现金付款，立即付款可以打九八折，但是分期付款需付全额。

格：噢，我明白了。

鲁：那么……您是打算用信用卡立即付款吗？

格：是的，没错。

鲁：这样的话，可以给您九八折。

格：太好了！

第8课 处理投诉

A 我要投诉……

(安娜的新车又坏了,她打电话到公司投诉。)

(鲁——鲁先生,安——安娜)

鲁:感谢您打电话到吉亨汽车销售公司,需要服务吗?

安:我要向你公司投诉。我一直信赖你们汽车的品质和你们的服务,但是这次我不得不改变我的看法。

鲁:感谢您对我们的认可。可究竟发生了什么使您改变了看法?

安:我刚把我的风神S30从修理厂开回来,可同样的问题又出现了。

鲁:又出现了?怎么可能呢?每一辆车都是仔细检查后才能交给顾客。

安:是的,那也是我想问你的问题。

鲁:也许它逃过了检验。

安:你要知道,我的车才买了三个月。

鲁:噢,十分抱歉。

安:我今天早上才换了新的变速器,但是它又坏了。这车子真差劲,我已经花了很多钱修它了。

鲁:我马上派维修员把您的车带回来仔细检查。如果是变速器的问题,我们将免费为您换一个新的,行吗?

安:谢谢!

鲁:不客气,而且我会联系我们的检验部门要求他们确保质量。

B 听到这些我很抱歉。

(布莱克从鲁志手上买了辆新车并订了一套四轮定位仪,现在他在投诉。)

(鲁——鲁先生,布——布莱克先生)

鲁:早上好,这里是吉亨汽车销售公司,有什么可以帮您的吗?

布:是的,我得向你公司提出投诉。这并不是一件令人高兴的事情。

鲁:噢,真遗憾听到此事,是什么事呢?

布:我前几天订购了一套四轮定位仪,等我收到后逐个检查时,我发现计算机屏幕一点信号都没有。

鲁:有没有看一看接线?

布:看了接线,那里面没问题。

鲁:那就奇怪了。我查一下并马上派人去你那里处理此事。

布:我可以退货吗?

鲁:抱歉我们不提供退货。如果我们有责任,我们会赔偿您的损失。我肯定那批货的装运一切都正常。

布:什么?真是荒唐!我要找你们经理谈。

鲁:请稍等,我会为您转接的。

附　录

第 9 课　用户反馈

A 您的车还好吧？

（鲁志正在给布莱克先生打电话，他的车上周来修过。）
（鲁——鲁先生，布——布莱克先生）

鲁：你好，这里是吉亨汽车公司。您是布莱克先生吗？
布：是的，我就是。
鲁：我打电话想知道您的车现在状况如何。
布：谢谢，自从修过之后，它很好。
鲁：很高兴听到您这么说，衷心希望这次修理没有给您带来不便。
布：谢谢您优质的服务。我相信贵公司一定会赚很多钱的。
鲁：给我们的顾客提供满意的服务一直是我们的宗旨。让我们作个市场调查吧，它会给我们一些启示的。请问：觉得我们的车如何？
布：我认为车的空间太小，以至于我总是不能在里面自由移动，而且喷漆做得不太好。
鲁：这是一个很好的建议，我会向经理汇报的，还有吗？
布：没有了，其他都很好。
鲁：谢谢您热情的回答。
布：这只是我个人的观点。
鲁：我们会做深入调查，谢谢您的建议，再见。
布：再见。

B 我们随时为您效劳。

（亨特先生已经买了一辆车，鲁先生正在打电话询问使用情况。）
（鲁——鲁先生，亨——亨特先生）

鲁：您好，我是吉亨汽车销售公司的售后服务顾问鲁志。请问您是 8 周前买了风神 AX7 汽车的亨特先生吗？
亨：是的，我就是。
鲁：亨特先生，感谢您购买我们的汽车。请问我可以花费您一点时间问您几个问题吗？
亨：可以。
鲁：请问您的车现在行驶了多少公里？
亨：我的车行驶了 1700 公里了。
鲁：车的一切状况都还好吗？
亨：是的，总体来说，我感觉这车动力强劲，我很满意。
鲁：您认为内饰怎么样？
亨：很宽敞、舒适而且实用，仪表盘清晰智能、操纵方便。
鲁：您认为性能如何？
亨：耗油不太高、安全配置很好，它的多点触摸中控屏、5G 无线网络、车载人工智能系统简直太酷了。

鲁：感谢您对我们品牌的肯定。您有什么不满意的地方吗？
亨：油漆做工不太满意、底盘不够高。
鲁：非常感谢您的反馈，我们将努力改进。友情提示，我们的车在行驶2500公里时需要做首保，主要项目有：更换机油、机滤、齿轮油、全车免费检查。
亨：好的。
鲁：如果车辆有任何问题和故障，请拨打87443578。我们将竭力为您服务。感谢您的合作，再见。
亨：再见。

第10课　维 修 接 待

A 我的车坏了。

（布什先生的车坏了，他正在给吉亨汽车维修厂打电话。王先生接听了他的电话。）
（王——前台接待员，布——布什先生）

王：早上好，这里是吉亨汽车维修厂，需要帮助吗？
布：是的，我的车坏了。
王：哦，很遗憾您的车坏了。能告诉我具体问题吗？
布：我想可能是发动机的故障，但是我不确定。我的车运行得不太好。我是指每次我起动时，发动机大约转了一分钟后，就像没有油一样噼啪响，然后就熄火了。
王：是哪年的哪款车？
布：是2019的丰田2.0自动档休闲车。
王：一般说来，这种车很少返修。车撞过吗？
布：没错，我曾撞上灯柱。您能安排维修人员过来维修吗？
王：没问题。请告诉我您的姓名、地址和电话号码。
布：好的，我的号码是13312345678，我在中山公园前门的大街上。我期待着您的到来，谢谢！
王：我知道了，我们的维修人员将在20分钟内赶到。您自己和车子要注意安全，再见。
布：谢谢！
王：不客气，再见。

B 我的车需要维修。

（格林太太来到吉亨汽车维修中心，前台接待员王先生接待了她。）
（王——前台接待员，格——格林太太）

王：早上好，夫人。需要帮助吗？
格：是的，我的车需要修理。这里可以吗？
王：当然，夫人。您的车怎么了？
格：3天前我听到我的车子乓乓响。
王：哦，是吗？是大声还是小声？
格：我想是小声。但是声音好像正变得有点大了。

王：哦？我们会为您检查的。
格：我明天能取吗？
王：我们会尽力的。但还要看是什么噪声问题。如果我们查出问题，我会为您打电话的。请填表登记并留下您的联系方式，我们会及时给您打电话的。
格：好的。
（第二天，格林太太想取车，她拨通了电话……）
王：您好，这里是吉亨汽车维修中心。
格：你好，我是蒂娜·格林，昨天我把车送去修理了。我想知道今天下午我能取车吗？
王：请稍等，我为您查一下。
格：好的，谢谢！
王：恩……格林太太，我们正要给您打电话。您的车是减振器坏了，需要换。
格：那么……
王：不用担心，我们的维修人员正在为您换新的减振器。
格：哦，太好了。我今天下午能取车吗？
王：没问题。
格：顺便问一下，要多少钱？
王：280 元。
格：谢谢！下午见！
王：再见。

第 11 课　汽车维护

A 您终于来了。

（布莱克先生刚给修理厂打了电话寻求帮助，现在他正在等待维修人员。）
（布——布莱克先生，维——维修人员）
布：你终于来了。
维：发生了什么问题？
布：我想我的车的制动出毛病了，因为当我的车低速行驶制动时，制动器就发出尖叫声。
维：让我看看。哦，制动片坏了。
布：是吗？
维：是的，我们必须把车拖回修理厂再换掉制动片。
布：没问题。
（一个小时后车子被拖回修理厂并换上了新制动片。）
维：好了，现在您可以试开一下车子。
布：好的，哦，尖叫声没了，谢谢您了。
维：不客气，能看看您的保修单吗？
布：当然可以，给。
维：哦，您的车的保修期已过，所更换的配件需要付款。
布：没关系。

维：请在这里签名，把这张维修单带到前台去交费。

布：感谢您及时赶到。

维：如果您的车有什么毛病，请给我们打电话，我们随时为您服务。

布：再次感谢！

维：十分荣幸为您效劳。

B 您的车要清洗打蜡吗？

（汤姆开着他的车子来到凯达修车行进行汽车维护，并且问了几个关于汽车清洁维护的常见问题。）

（王——维修员王先生，汤——汤姆）

王：你好，先生。能为您做点什么吗？

汤：我想做一个5000km基础维护。

王：没问题。请在我们的顾客休息厅休息等候。我马上开始。

汤：谢谢！

（半小时后。）

王：先生，您的车的维护已经做完。但是您的车很脏，要清洗打蜡吗？

汤：好的，顺便问一下，您能告诉我清洗和打蜡方法吗？

王：首先，洗掉车子表面的浮尘和沙子，这样的话车子不会被划伤。

汤：我用什么洗呢？如何洗？

王：只能用干净的海绵和汽车洗涤剂来洗车身。首先上下洗，然后前后洗，车轮最后洗。

汤：用什么擦干它？

王：用一块特殊的抛光布。如果您用普通的布来擦，布的绒毛将附着在车表面上。

汤：完了之后，我又该如何做？

王：用不同的蜡来美化车身和皮革座椅。车身蜡分为两种：硬蜡和软蜡。一般说来硬蜡要持久一些。

汤：什么时候上蜡，我该特别注意些什么？

王：确保没有灰尘在车的表面。为了避免浪费太多的蜡，打上薄薄的一层就可以了。

汤：我需要等到蜡干了再用海绵擦干它吗？

王：当然。实际上，只要按照说明使用就行了。

汤：非常感谢。

第12课 汽车保险

A 您要买保险吗？

（迪克想为他的车买份保险，他向约翰请教了一些关于保险的事……）

（迪——迪克，约——约翰，接——接待员，鲍——鲍博）

迪：你好，约翰，我想买份车险，你有什么好主意？

约：你可以咨询中国人民保险公司。

迪：他们有车险吗？

约：据我所知，他们为所有的车辆提供保险。
迪：他们的保费很低吗？
约：不是很低，但很合理，我觉得他们的服务很好。
迪：中国人民保险公司能为汽车提供哪些保险？
约：我不太清楚，我给你他们的电话，你可以打电话咨询。
迪：谢谢，我会打给他们的。
（铃，铃……）
接：下午好，中国人民保险公司，有什么我能帮您吗？
迪：下午好，我想为我的车买份保险。我能和保险代理谈下吗？
接：请等一下，我马上为您转接一位保险代理。
鲍：你好，我是鲍博，我有什么能帮您的吗？
迪：你好，我想要为我的车买份保险。
鲍：好的，您的车是什么型号的？
迪：是一辆风神S30，我去年买的。
鲍：您想要哪种免赔率的？我们一般是25%。
迪：这是什么意思？
鲍：免赔率是指保险费不会保的部分。举个例子，如果修理费是1000元，免赔率是25%，那么保险费将只赔750元。
迪：哦，我明白。
鲍：我们还保第三者责任险和财产损失险。
迪：那这些需要多少钱？
鲍：给我几分钟，让我算一下。
迪：好的。
鲍：保险费是税前1250元每年。
迪：有点贵。
鲍：我们的费率已经很低了。
迪：好吧，让我考虑下。
鲍：当然可以，如果您有空的话，您最好来我们的公司，我将会向您提供一些保险的资料。
迪：我会接受您的建议的。
鲍：如果您想知道更详细的汽车保险，您也可以给我打电话。我的电话号码是87294538。
迪：您真是热心。
鲍：这是我的荣幸。
迪：好吧，保险问题就谈到这里。祝您今天愉快。
鲍：好的，再见。
迪：再见。

B 我想了解一下汽车保险。

（威廉想为他的车买份保险，张先生在中国人民保险公司接待了他……）
（威—威廉先生，张—保险代理张先生）

威：有人在吗？
张：是的，有什么能为您服务吗？
威：我想在你们公司投保。我想知道一些关于保险的事情。
张：这是我的荣幸，请讲。
威：最近，我买了一辆新车，不幸的是，我在5天前遇到了一场车祸。我想为我的车买份保险。
张：哦，我明白了。
威：我应该买什么样的险种？
张：是私家车吗？
威：是的，针对私家车，贵公司将为我提供哪些险种？
张：您介意我询问您一些问题吗？
威：不介意，请讲。
张：您多大年龄，是做什么的？
威：我今年35岁，是一名教师。
张：您经常开车吗？
威：有时。
张：针对您的情况，我们建议您买"经济保险"方案——交强险+车损险+第三者责任险+不计免赔险。
威：保险费是多少？
张：给我几分钟计算保费。
威：好的。
张：保费是2100元每年。
威：你们的价钱高了些。
张：我们可以适当降低。具体的事宜，保险单写得非常清楚。
威：那贵公司能先给我提供一份吗？我好回去和家人商量。
张：当然可以，我马上拿给您。
威：谢谢。
张：给您吧。
威：这些目录我想带走。
张：好啊，请便。
威：我还想把这些价格单子带走。
张：随便你拿。这是我的名片，如果您有什么不懂的地方，请给我打电话。
威：好的。
张：您有名片吗？
威：有，在这里。
张：谢谢。
威：我希望能和您合作，下次见。
张：下次见。

附录 C 汽车专业词汇

A

acceleration 加速度
accelerator pedal 加速踏板
accessory system 辅助系统
active safety 主动安全
adjustable seats 可调节座椅
adjustable steering column 可调转向柱
agricultural vehicle 农用车
air cleaner 空气滤清器
air cooled 风冷
air filtration system 空气过滤系统
airbags 安全气囊
air-conditioning system 空调系统
alloy 合金
all-wheel-drive system 四轮驱动系统
alternator 交流发电机
aluminum chassis 铝合金底盘
aluminum pedals 铝制踏板
AM 调幅
ambulance 救护车
ammeter 电流表
anchor 安装
angle of approach 接近角
angle of departure 离去角
angle 角度
Anti-Lock Braking System（ABS）防抱死制动系统
arm rest 臂枕
arrange 排列
arrangement 排列
articulated vehicle 铰接车、拖车
audio system 音频系统
automatic dimming rear-mirror 自动调光后视镜
automatic gears 自动档
automatic transmission 自动变速器
automatic window 自动窗
automobile 汽车
auxiliary 辅助的
axle housing 轴壳

B

battery 蓄电池
beam 防擦条
bearing 轴承
bluetooth hands free link 蓝牙免提系统
body 车身
Brake Assist（BA）制动辅助系统
brake disk 制动盘
brake master cylinder 制动总泵
brake drum 制动鼓
brake booster 制动助力器
brake valve 制动组合阀
brake pedal 制动踏板
brake 制动
bucket tappet 挺柱
bumpers 保险杠

C

cabin 车厢
camshaft sprocket 凸轮轴齿形带轮
camshaft 凸轮轴
capacity 容量
car heater 汽车暖风
carburetor 化油器
carpet 脚垫
center armrest 中央扶手
center bearing 中心轴
center resistor 中央电阻

centimeter (cm) 厘米
charging system 充电系统
chassis 底盘
check 检查
child safety rear door locks 儿童后门安全门锁
cigar lighter 点烟器
circulate 循环
circuit 电路
cleaner 清洁器
climbing ability 爬坡能力
clutch 离合器
clutch pedal 离合器踏板
coach 旅游轿车
coil spring 螺旋弹簧
comfort equipment 舒适配置
commercial vehicle 商用车
compartment 分隔间，厢室
component 零件，组成件
compression 压缩
compression ratio 压缩比
condenser 电容器
connecting rod 连杆
Constant Speed Fuel Consumption 等速油耗
consumption 消耗
convenience equipment 方便配置
convertible 折叠敞篷轿车，敞篷的
coolant pump 冷却水泵
coolant 冷却剂
cooling system 冷却系统
configuration 配置
counterweights 配重
coupe 双人轿车
covering 遮盖物
crane car 吊车
crankshaft sprocket 曲轴齿形带轮
crankshaft 曲轴
crossmember 横梁
cubic centimeter (cm^3) 立方厘米
cup holders fixed 固定杯架

curb weight 整备质量
cycle 循环
cylinder block 气缸体
cylinder head 气缸盖
cylinder 气缸

D

dashboard 仪表盘
Daytime Running Lights (DRL) 日间行车灯
device 装置
diesel fuel 柴油
differential 差速器
dimension 尺寸
directional stability 方向稳定性
displacement 排量
distribute 分配
distributor 分电器
door ajar warning 门未关紧提示
door lock switch 门锁开关
drive 行驶
drive axle 驱动桥
driving belt 传动带
driving power 驱动力
driving shaft 传动轴
driving system 行驶系统
drum brake 制动鼓

E

ECM 电子控制模块
electrical system 电气系统
electrical 电气的
electricity 电
Electronic Brake Distribution (EBD) 电子制动力分配系统
Electronic Control Unit (ECU) 电子控制单元
energy 能源
engine room 发动机室
engine 发动机
exhaust manifold 排气歧管

exterior equipment 外饰
exterior 外部
exhaust 排气

F

feature 特征
filtration 过滤
final drive 主减速器
fire engine 消防车
flat arrangement 平面排列
floor mat 地板垫
fly wheel 飞轮
FM 调频
frame 车架
front fender 前翼板
front bumper 前保险杠杆
front cover 前盖
front differential 前差速器
front drive shaft 前驱动轴
front suspension 前悬架
fuel consumption 油耗
fuel system 燃油系统
fuel tank 燃油箱
fuel-injection unit 喷油器
fuel 燃料
fuel filter 燃油过滤器
function 功能

G

gasoline 汽油
gasoline engine 汽油发动机
gear 齿轮，装置
gear box 变速器
glove compartment 杂物箱
goods 货物
gram (g) 克
gross vehicle weight 汽车总质量
ground clearance 最小离地间隙

H

half axle 半轴
hand controlled window 手动窗
handle 把手
hanger 支架
head restraint 安全头枕
heart 心脏
head-light 前照灯
heavy vehicle 重型车
height 高度
hydrogen-power 氢动力
hood 罩
horn button 喇叭按钮
horn relay 喇叭继电器
horn 喇叭

I

ignite 点火
ignition coil 点火线圈
ignition distributor 点火分电器
ignition switch 点火开关
ignition 点火
illuminated entry system 进车照明系统
immobilizer theft-deterrent system 防盗系统
immobilizer 防盗锁止系统
indicator 指标
injector 喷油器
inline 直列式
initiate 起动
instrument panel 仪表盘
intake manifold 进气歧管
intake 进气
interior 内部
interior decoration 内饰
interior equipment 内饰
interior height 室内高
interior length 室内长
interior width 室内宽

J

jeep 吉普车

K

kilogram (kg) 千克
kiloliter (kL) 千升
kilometer (km) 千米
kilometer/per hour (km/h) 千米/每小时
kilowatt (kW) 千瓦
driver knee airbags 驾驶人膝盖安全气囊

L

lamp post 灯柱
leaf springs 钢板弹簧
leather-wrapped steering wheel 真皮转向盘
length 长度
lighting system 照明系统
lights switch 灯光开关
light 灯
liquid cooled 水冷
liter (L) 升，公升
load 载荷
location 位置
locked condition 锁死状态
locked up 锁死
low voltage wire 低压导线
lower control arm 下控制臂
luggage 行李
lubrication system 润滑系统

M

magnetic switch 电磁开关
main-bearing cap 主轴承盖
main-bearing 主轴承
main fuse 主熔断丝
maintain 维护
manual gears 手动档

manual transmission 手动变速器
map lamp 阅读灯
maximum 最大的
maximum output 最大功率
maximum speed 最高车速
maximum torque 最大转矩
maximum turning radius 最大转弯半径
measure 测量
metallic paint 金属漆
meter (m) 米
millimeter (mm) 毫米
mix 混合
mixture 混合物
mixer truck 搅拌车
muffler 消声器
multi-reflector halogen headlights 多反射卤素前照灯
motor 电动机

N

Navigation system with Real Time Traffic Information (NRTTI) 驾驶导航系统

O

off-road vehicle 越野车
oil pan 油底壳
oil pump 机油泵
oil seal 油封
one-touch power sunroof 一触式电动天窗
outlets 电源插座
output 功率
overall height 总高
overall length 总长
overall width 总宽
overhang front 前悬
overhang rear 后悬
OHC 顶置凸轮轴
OHV 顶置气门

P

parameter 参数
Park Distance Control（PDC）停车距离控制系统
parking brake lever 驻车制动拉杆
parking light 驻车灯
parts 零件
passage 通道
passenger 乘客
passive safety 被动安全
performance 性能
pickup vehicle 货车（皮卡车）
piston 活塞
policecar 警车
portion 部分
power door locks 电动门锁
power exterior mirror 电动后视镜
power steering 动力转向
power steering wheel 动力转向盘
power steering 助力转向
power train 传动系统
power window 电动车窗
power 动力
pressure 压力
produce 产生
property safety 财产安全
protective 保护的
protect 保护
provide 提供
pushrod 推杆
pump 泵

R

radiator 散热器
radius rod 纵向推力杆
rear 后部
rear bumper 后保险杠
rear differential box 后差速器
rear drive shaft 后驱动轴
rear fender 后翼板
rear shackle 后吊耳
rear suspension 后悬架，后桥
rearview mirror 后视镜
recreational vehicle 旅行车
refrigerator truck 冷藏车
regulator 电压调节器
remote key 遥控钥匙
resistant wire 高压线
resistor 电阻器
reverse parking sensors 倒车感应器
roof 顶篷
room lamp 顶灯
rotate 旋转
Run-Flat Tires 零胎压继续行驶
rocker arm 摇臂
Road Cycle Fuel Consumption 道路循环油耗

S

safety devices 安全装置
safety equipment 安全配置
Satellite-Linked Navigation System 卫星导航系统
seat belts 安全带
seat 座椅
second（sec）秒
sedan 轿车
security equipment 安全配置
shape 形状
shift lever 变速杆
shock absorber 减振器
shock 振动
side airbags 侧安全气囊
side curtain airbags 侧窗安全气囊
snowplow 铲雪车
solar 太阳能
solve 解决
spare parts 备件

spare tire 备胎
spark plug 火花塞
speaker 扩音器
special polish rag 特殊的抛光布
specification 说明，说明书，规范
speed meter 速度表
speed 速度
spring 弹簧
stabilizer bar 稳定杆
starter 起动机
starter relay 发动机继电器
starting 发动机
starting motor 起动电动机
start up 点火起动
starter drive gear 起动驱动齿轮
starting system 起动系统
station wagon 旅行车
steering arm 转向臂
steering knuckle 转向节
steering system 转向系统
steer 转向
steering gear 转向器
steering shaft 转向轴
steering shock absorber 转向减振器
steering wheel 转向盘
storage pocket 杂物格
store 存储
stroke 冲程
structure 结构
stub axle 销轴
sun roof 活动车顶
sun visor 遮阳板
support 支撑
surround 环绕
suspension member 悬架总成
suspension 悬架
SUV 运动型多功能车
swing 摆动
switch 开关

T

tachometer 转速表
tail-light 尾灯
tank 油箱
technical data 技术参数
temperature 温度
term 术语
the brake pads 制动块
throttle-body 节气门体
tipping vehicles 自卸车
Tire Pressure Monitoring System (TPMS) 轮胎压力监测系统
tire 轮胎
timing 正时
toothed timing belt 齿形正时带
torque 转矩
total displacement 总排量
track front 前轮距
track rear 后轮距
tractor 拖拉机
trailing arm 纵臂
transmission 变速器
trouble 故障
truck 货车
trunk lid 行李厢盖
trunk room 行李厢
trunk/cargo space 行李厢容积
turbocharging 涡轮增压

U

universal joint 万向节

V

vacuum 真空
valve cover 气门室罩
valve lifter 气门挺柱
valve 气门
van 厢式货车

Vehicle Stability Assist（VSA）车身稳定辅助装置
vehicle 汽车
vinyl 乙烯树脂
voltage regulator 电压调节器
volt（V）伏

W

warning system 报警系统
water sprinkler 洒水车
watt（W）瓦
weight 质量
wheel alignment 四轮定位仪
wheel rim 轮毂
wheelbase 轴距
wheel 轮子
width 宽度
window defroster 后窗除霜器
wiper 刮水器

附录 D 常用词汇

A

a bunch of 一束
ability 能力
a range of 很多的
a set of 一套
a thin layer 薄薄一层
absorb 吸收
accept 接受
accessory 附件
according to 按照，根据
acquaintance 熟人
active 主动的
active safety 主动安全
additional 额外的
advanced 先进的
advantage 优势
after all 毕竟，究竟
agent 代理
aggressive 积极的，主动的
agree with 同意
air conditioner 空调
all risk 全险
allow 允许
amount 数量
annually 每年
appearance 外表
application 应用
appointment 预约
appreciate 感谢
arrange 安排
arrival 到达
as a matter of fact 事实上
as follows 如下

at all 根本
at present 现在
attractive 吸引人的
auto 汽车
automatic 自动的
available 可得到的

B

bank transfer 银行汇款
bargain 交易
basic 基本的
be anxious to 急于……
be applied to 应用于……
be at fault 有过错
be aware of 意识到
be called 称为
be capable of 能够
be classified as 归类为
be classified into 可分成
be equipped with 配备……
be forced to 被迫
be known as 以……著名，被认为是
be made up of 由……组成
be raised/lowered 升/降
be related to 与……有关
beautify 美化
belong to 属于
benefit 利益
bet 打赌
break down 损坏，出故障
briefly 简洁地
budget 预算
business card 名片
by credit card 用信用卡

C

calculate 计算
car detergent 汽车清洗剂
cargo 货物
cash 现金
catalog 目录，商品目录
cause 引起
chance 机会
change one's mind 改变想法
changeable 易变的
characterize 表现……特性
charge for 收……费
check 检查
check over 仔细检查
choice 选择
cinematic 电影院般的
classification 类别
collect 收集
come out 出来
come over 过来
come to an end 过期了
comfort 舒适
common 共同，常见的
communicate 交流
company 公司
compare 对比
compel 强迫
competitive 有竞争力的（价格）
complain 投诉/抱怨
complete with 连同……
composition 组成部分
condition 状况
confidence 信心
connection 接头
consider 考虑
consist of 由……组成
constant 不变的
consult 参考，查阅，咨询
consumption 消耗
contain 包含
contract 合同
control 控制
convenience 方便
convenient 方便的
cooperate with 与……合作
cooperation 合作
costs 费用
courage 勇气
crash 碰撞，事故
credit card 信用卡
customer 客户
customer lounge 顾客休息厅

D

dashboard 仪表盘
deal with 应对，处理
decision 决定
deductible（尤指税收、应纳税的收入中）可扣除的
definitely 肯定地，明确地
department 部门
depend 依靠，取决于
depend on 依据，取决于
describe 描述
design 设计
desk clerk 接待员
detail 细节，详情
determine 决定
develop 开发
device 装置
dial 拨打电话
difference 不同
differences between 与……不同
dimension 尺寸
directions 说明书
directly 直接地
discontent 不满意

discount 折扣
discuss 讨论
distinguishing 显著的
disturb 打扰
divide into 分为
down installment 首付款
drive at low speed 低速驾驶
dry 弄干
durable 耐用的

E

economy 经济
economically efficiency 经济地效率
emergency 紧急情况
enjoy doing 喜欢做某事……
ensure 确保
entertainment 娱乐
entry 进入
equip 配备
escape 逃避
essential 必要的
even if 即使
examine 检查，调试
expect 期待
expectation 期待
explain 解说
explanation 讲解
express 表达
extend 伸展

F

failure 故障，失败
favor 好感
feature 配置
features 设施
feedback 反馈意见
fetch 取回
fill paperwork 填表登记
first of all 首先

flexible 灵活的
fluff 绒毛
flush away 冲洗去
for ages 很长时间
for fear of 为避免
for free 免费
for... purpose 以……为目的
force 强迫
frankly 坦率地
further 进一步地

G

garage 修理厂
gear 齿轮，装置
general question 一般疑问句
generally speaking 一般说来
get on to 联系
give up 放弃
go ahead 继续
grasp 抓住
guarantee 保证

H

harmonious 和谐的
have in mind 想到，留意
heart and soul 全心全意
hesitate 犹豫
hobby 爱好
hold 容纳
hold the line 请稍等（打电话）

I

important 重要的
in a poor condition 状况不佳
in cash 用现金
in detail 详细地
in order to 为了
in our daily life 在我们的日常生活中
in poor condition 在恶劣的条件下

in the back of 在……的后部
in the front of 在……的前部
include 包括
inconvenience 不方便
indirectly 间接地
inform 告知
injured 受伤的
information 信息
insist on 坚持
inspection 检验
installment 分期付款
insurance 保险单
insurance agent 保险代理
Insurance Company 保险公司
insurance policy 保险单
insure 保险，投保
intend to 打算
interrupt 打扰
introduce 介绍（动词）
introduction 介绍（名词）

J

judge 判断

K

keep in touch with 保持联系
keep promise 信守承诺
kill time 消磨时间

L

lack 缺乏
lawyer 律师
limited 有限的
look around 随便看看
look for 寻找
look forward to 期待
look like 看起来像
lose control of 失控

M

main 主要的
maintain 维修
maintaining sheet 维修单
maintenance 维护
make 样式，牌子，品牌
make a complaint 投诉
make good 补偿
make phone call 打电话
make up one's mind 下定决心
manager 经理
market research 市场调查
marvelous 好极了
maximum 最大的
mechanic 技术工人
medium 中型的
mileage 英里数
model 样式

N

name card 名片
necessary 必要的
net 全额

O

observe 观察
obtain 获得
occupant 乘客
occupation 职业
office 办公室
on earth 究竟
on looker 旁观者
on the whole 大体上
one another 互相
operation 操作
opinion 观点
or so 大约
order 订购

order form 订货单
outlook 外观
outstanding 杰出的
overcome 克服
overvalue 超值

P

paperwork 文书工作
park 停车
patiently 耐心地
pay 付款
persuade 劝说
pick up 拿到
plan 计划
pleasant surprise 惊喜
point out 指出
policy 政策
polite 礼貌
postpone 推迟
power 动力
powerful 强劲的
practical 实用的
predestination 缘分
prefer 更喜欢
premium 保险费
premise 前提
prepare 准备
prevent from 防止……免于
price list 价格表
principle 原则
privacy 隐私
private 私有的
probably 可能地
professional 专业的
professionally 专业地
promise 承诺
promotion 促销
prompt 及时的，迅速的
protect 保护（动词）

protection 保护（名词）
protective 保护的
provide 提供
put through 接通

Q

quality 质量

R

rag 布块
real bargain 合算的交易
realistic 现实的
reasonable 合理的
receive 接待
recent 最近的
recommend 推荐
refer to 涉及
refuse 拒绝
regard 看待
rely 信任
rely on 信赖
remote 遥远的
repair 修理
repair process 维修过程
repairs 修理费
repeatedly 重复地
replace 替换，更换
reply 答复
report 报告
restraint 抑制
return 退还
ridiculous 不可思议的
rights 权利
ring 打电话
risk 险别
risks covered 保险范围
road condition 路况
room 空间
roomy 宽敞的

rub 擦
run 运行

S

safety 安全
sale 销售
sales contract 销售合同
sales drive 促销
sales tax 营业税
salesman 销售员
satisfactory 满意的
science 科学
scratch 擦伤
seamless 无缝隙的
sedan 小轿车
seldom 很少
send out 发出
serve 服务，招待
set 处理
set out 出发
shipment 装货
sign 签署
sign the contract 签合同
signal 信号
since 既然
smoothly 顺利地
spacious 宽敞的
special 特殊的
specific question 特殊疑问句
sponge 海绵
sputter 噼啪声
squeal 尖叫
stand 立场
stand for 代表
standard 标准的，标准
stare at 盯着
stick to 附着
such as 例如
suggestion 建议

suit 适合
supplemental 补充的
suppose 假使
surface 表面

T

take an interest in 对……有兴趣
take it easy 别急
take measure 采取措施
take opportunity 抓住机会
take your point 同意
take your time 从容做……
talk over 详尽地商议
technology 技术
tell the truth 说实话
tend to 转到
terms of payment 付款方式
test 测试
the front desk 前台
the guarantee of ……的保证
the other day 前几天
the third part liability 第三者责任险
think over 仔细考虑
think about 考虑
tough 坚固的
traffic regulation 交规
treat with 应付
try one's best 尽力

U

unpleasant 不愉快的
unreasonable 不讲理的

V

various kinds of 各种各样的
vehicle 车辆，运载工具

W

warm-hearted 热情的

warranty 保修单
warranty certificate 保修卡
wash and wax 清洗和打蜡
wax 打蜡
well-sighted 好看的
wise 明智的

with the development of 随着……的发展
worn 破旧
worn out 磨损，很旧
would like to 愿意
write down 记下

参考文献

[1] 宋建桐,王晓平. 汽车英语[M]. 北京:外文出版社,2007.
[2] 黄立新. 汽车专业英语[M]. 西安:西安电子科技大学出版社,2006.
[3] 刘渝. 汽车维修职场英语[M]. 重庆:重庆大学出版社,2006.
[4] 王运泉. 汽车商务英语[M]. 北京:人民交通出版社,2004.
[5] 黄会明,倪勇. 汽车4S企业管理与业务接待[M]. 北京:机械工业出版社,2014.
[6] 张金柱. 图解英汉汽车实用词典[M]. 北京:化学工业出版社,2014.
[7] 郑毅. 汽车英语[M]. 北京:外语教学与研究出版社,2013.